Beginning Swift

Master the fundamentals of programming in Swift 4

Rob Kerr
Kåre Morstøl

BIRMINGHAM - MUMBAI

D1352278

Beginning Swift

Acquisitions Editor: Aditya Date
Content Development Editor: Taabish Khan
Production Coordinator: Vishal Pawar

First published: July 2018

Production reference: 1250718

Published by Packt Publishing Ltd.
Livery Place
35 Livery Street
Birmingham B3 2PB, UK.

ISBN 978-1-78953-431-3

www.packtpub.com

`mapt.io`

Mapt is an online digital library that gives you full access to over 5,000 books and videos, as well as industry leading tools to help you plan your personal development and advance your career. For more information, please visit our website.

Why Subscribe?

- Spend less time learning and more time coding with practical eBooks and Videos from over 4,000 industry professionals

- Learn better with Skill Plans built especially for you

- Get a free eBook or video every month

- Mapt is fully searchable

- Copy and paste, print, and bookmark content

PacktPub.com

Did you know that Packt offers eBook versions of every book published, with PDF and ePub files available? You can upgrade to the eBook version at `www.PacktPub.com` and as a print book customer, you are entitled to a discount on the eBook copy. Get in touch with us at `service@packtpub.com` for more details.

At `www.PacktPub.com`, you can also read a collection of free technical articles, sign up for a range of free newsletters, and receive exclusive discounts and offers on Packt books and eBooks.

Contributors

About the Authors

Rob Kerr is a mobile software architect based in United States. He has been working professionally with Swift since its introduction, delivering applications to the public App Store and through enterprise distribution. His current focus is developing state-of-the-art iOS applications using Swift in the IoT space.

Kåre Morstøl is an independent software developer from Norway, with a bachelor's degree in software development. He has programmed almost exclusively in Swift since it was announced. He thinks it's a great language that is continually getting better.

Packt is Searching for Authors Like You

If you're interested in becoming an author for Packt, please visit `authors.packtpub.com` and apply today. We have worked with thousands of developers and tech professionals, just like you, to help them share their insight with the global tech community. You can make a general application, apply for a specific hot topic that we are recruiting an author for, or submit your own idea.

Table of Contents

Preface

Swift is a multi-paradigm language. It has expressive features familiar to those used to working with modern functional languages, whilst also keeping the object-oriented features of Objective-C. Swift vastly streamlines the developer experience, and Apple's Xcode playground is a real game-changer.

The book begins by teaching you the basic syntax and structure of Swift, and how to correctly structure and architect software using Swift. It then builds expertise in the core Swift standard library you will need to understand to complete real-world Swift programming projects. We will work through concepts such as operators, branching and loop structures, functions, classes, structs, collections, and strings. We end the book with a brief look at functional programming and lazy operations.

After reading and understanding this book, you will be well-prepared to begin developing native end-user applications for iOS or macOS, or to develop server-side (backend) application and web services using Swift on Linux.

What This Book Covers

Lesson 1, Swift Basics, covers the fundamentals of using the Swift programming language. In this lesson, you'll learn basic Swift syntax and program structure. You'll also learn how to use Swift built-in data types and enums, and how to declare and use Swift variables and constants.

Lesson 2, Swift Operators and Control Flow, shows you how to use the fundamental flow control structures and language elements that form the building blocks of Swift programs. We will specifically cover operators, branching statements, and loops in this lesson.

Lesson 3, Functions, Classes, and Structs, teaches you how to develop fully featured Swift functions, catch unexpected errors, and use asynchronous programming paradigms. You'll learn how to create your own data types, and create object-oriented applications using classes and structs.

Lesson 4, Collections, shows you how to work with Swift's collections, such as arrays, sets, and dictionaries.

Lesson 5, Strings, covers Swift strings in detail. We will create and use strings and substrings, and see the various common operations available for them.

Lesson 6, Functional Programming and Lazy Operations, introduces functional programming and explains what lazy operations are. We will end with an important but often overlooked topic—writing Swifty code.

The first three lessons are written by *Rob Kerr*, and lessons 4-6 are written by *Kåre Morstøl*.

What You Need for This Book

This book will require the following hardware:

- A Mac computer capable of running macOS Sierra 10.12.6+
- An internet connection

Please ensure you have the following software installed on your machine:

- Operating system: macOS Sierra 10.12.6+
- Xcode 9.1
- Safari browser

Who This Book Is For

This book is ideal for developers seeking fundamental Swift programming skills, in preparation for learning to develop native applications for iOS or macOS. No prior Swift knowledge is expected but object-oriented programming experience is desirable.

You should have basic working knowledge of computer programming in a procedural/ object-oriented language, such as Objective-C, BASIC, C++, Python, Java, or JavaScript.

Conventions

In this book, you will find a number of text styles that distinguish between different kinds of information. Here are some examples of these styles and an explanation of their meaning.

Code words *in text* are shown as follows: "Finally, use the console `print` function to output the content of each error variable."

Folder names, filenames, file extensions, pathnames, include file names in text are shown as follows: "Launch Xcode as before, and create a new playground named `Create a Variable.playground`."

A block of code is set as follows:

```
let name = "John Doe"
var address = "201 Main Street"
print("\(name) lives at \(address)")
```

New terms and important words are shown in bold. Words that you see on the screen, for example, in menus or dialog boxes, appear in the text like this: "Choose **Blank** as the playground template, and then press the **Next** button."

Important new **programming terms** are shown in bold. *Conceptual terms* are shown in italics.

 Important additional details about a topic appear like this, as in a sidebar.

 Important notes, tips, and tricks appear like this.

Reader Feedback

Feedback from our readers is always welcome. Let us know what you think about this book—what you liked or disliked. Reader feedback is important for us as it helps us develop titles that you will really get the most out of.

To send us general feedback, simply e-mail `feedback@packtpub.com`, and mention the book's title in the subject of your message.

If there is a topic that you have expertise in and you are interested in either writing or contributing to a book, see our author guide at `www.packtpub.com/authors`.

Customer Support

Now that you are the proud owner of a Packt book, we have a number of things to help you to get the most from your purchase.

Downloading the Example Code

You can download the example code files from your account at `http://www.packtpub.com` for all the Packt Publishing books you have purchased. If you purchased this book elsewhere, you can visit `http://www.packtpub.com/support` and register to have the files e-mailed directly to you.

Errata

Although we have taken every care to ensure the accuracy of our content, mistakes do happen. If you find a mistake in one of our books—maybe a mistake in the text or the code—we would be grateful if you could report this to us. By doing so, you can save other readers from frustration and help us improve subsequent versions of this book. If you find any errata, please report them by visiting `http://www.packtpub.com/submit-errata`, selecting your book, clicking on the **Errata Submission Form** link, and entering the details of your errata. Once your errata are verified, your submission will be accepted and the errata will be uploaded to our website or added to any list of existing errata under the Errata section of that title.

To view the previously submitted errata, go to `https://www.packtpub.com/books/content/support` and enter the name of the book in the search field. The required information will appear under the **Errata** section.

Piracy

Piracy of copyrighted material on the Internet is an ongoing problem across all media. At Packt, we take the protection of our copyright and licenses very seriously. If you come across any illegal copies of our works in any form on the Internet, please provide us with the location address or website name immediately so that we can pursue a remedy.

Please contact us at copyright@packtpub.com with a link to the suspected pirated material.

We appreciate your help in protecting our authors and our ability to bring you valuable content.

Questions

If you have a problem with any aspect of this book, you can contact us at questions@packtpub.com, and we will do our best to address the problem.

1
Swift Basics

Swift is a relatively new programming language designed by Apple Inc., and was initially made available to Apple developers in 2014 — primarily intended as a replacement for the aging Objective-C language that was the foundation of OS X and iOS software development at the time.

Unlike many object-oriented languages, which are based on older procedural languages — for example, C++ and Objective-C are based on C — Swift was designed from the ground up as a new, modern, object-oriented language that makes programming faster and easier, and helps developers produce expressive code that's less prone to errors than many languages.

While not based on an older language, Swift, in the words of its chief architect, Chris Lattner, *"was inspired by drawing ideas from Objective-C, Rust, Haskell, Ruby, Python, C#, CLU, and far too many others to list."* (Chris Lattner home page: `http://nondot.org/sabre/`).

Swift was initially a proprietary language, but was made open source software in December 2015 as of its version 2.2. While Swift remains primarily used by developers targeting the Apple macOS and iOS platforms, Swift is also fully supported on Linux, and there are unofficial ports under development for Windows as well.

The objective of this lesson is to learn the fundamentals of using the Swift programming language. In this lesson, you'll learn basic Swift syntax and program structure. You'll also learn how to use Swift built-in data types and enums, and how to declare and use Swift variables and constants. Let's get started.

Lesson objectives

By the end of this lesson, you will be able to:

- Explain the program structure and syntax of Swift programs
- Declare and use Swift variables and constants
- Use the various built-in Swift data types
- Use the Swift enum language syntax

Swift Program Structure

In this first section, we'll look at the basic language syntax for Swift, and you'll write your first fully functional Swift program.

Like many modern programming languages, Swift draws its most basic syntax from the programming language C. If you have previous programming experience in other C-inspired languages, such as C++, Java, C#, Objective-C, or PHP, many aspects of Swift will seem familiar, and many Swift concepts you will probably find quite familiar.

We can say the following about Swift's basic syntax:

- Programs are made up of statements, executed sequentially
- More than one statement are allowed per editor line when separated by a semicolon (;)
- Units of work in Swift are modularized using functions and organized into types
- Functions accept one or more parameters, and return values
- Single and multiline comments follow the same syntax as in C++ and Java
- Swift data type names and usage are similar to that in Java, C#, and C++
- Swift has the concept of named variables, which are mutable, and named constants, which are immutable
- Swift has both struct and class semantics, as do C++ and C#

If you have prior experience in other C-inspired languages, such as Java, C#, or C++, Swift has some improvements and differences that will take some time and practice for you to become accustomed to:

- Semicolons are *not required* at the end of statements — except when used to separate multiple statements typed on the same line in a source file.

- Swift has no `main()` method to serve as the program's starting point when the operating system loads the application. Swift programs begin at the first line of code of the program's source file — as is the case in most interpreted languages.

- Functions in Swift place the function return at the right-hand side of the function declaration, rather than the left.

- Function parameter declaration syntax is inspired by Objective-C, which is quite different and often at first confusing for Java, C#, and C++ developers.

- The difference between a struct and a class in Swift is similar to what we have in C# (value type versus reference type), but not the same as in C++ (both are the same, except struct members are public by default).

For those coming to Swift from Java, C++, C#, and similar languages, your previous experience with other C-inspired languages will help accelerate your progress learning Swift. However, be sure to study the language syntax carefully and be on the lookout for subtle differences.

Hello, World!

When learning a new language, it's traditional for a first program to make sure the development environment is installed and properly configured by writing a program that outputs something to the screen. That's what we'll do next.

Now, let's use an Xcode playground to create a simple Swift program to display the string *Hello, World* to the playground console, by following these steps:

1. Begin by launching Xcode. You should be presented with a **Welcome to Xcode** screen with the following commands listed on the left:

    1. **Get started with a playground**

    2. **Create a new Xcode project**

    3. **Clone an existing project**

2. Since we'll be writing code but not building an application in this lesson, choose the **Get started with a playground** option to open an interactive code window.

 Xcode playgrounds are provided to allow developers to quickly experiment with Swift code. In addition to learning Swift, as we are in this lesson, you can use playgrounds to develop functions and test whether a specific fragment of Swift code will do what you expect.

3. Choose **Blank** as the playground template, and then press the **Next** button.

4. Next, Xcode will prompt where to save the playground. This will save your code in a file with a playground file extension. Name the playground HelloWorld, and save it to your desktop.

5. When Xcode creates a new playground, it adds some default code to the editing window. Press ⌘A on your keyboard and then the *Delete* key on the keyboard to delete the sample code.

6. In the now-blank editor window, add the following two lines of code:

```
let message = "Hello, World."
print(message)
```

Congratulations! You've just written your first Swift program. If you see the text **Hello, World.** output in the bottom pane of the playground window, your program has worked.

Before we move on, let's look at the structure of the playground window:

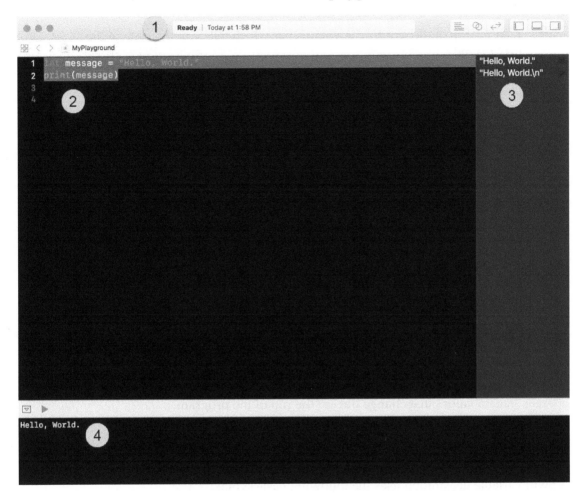

Note the following regions in the playground window, as indicated by the numbers within the red circles:

- **1**: At the top of the window is a status bar which tells you the state of the playground.
- **2**: The editing pane of the window is where you type the code to run in the playground.
- **3**: The right-hand pane of the playground window shows information about the effect of each line of code. In this simple program, it shows the value `message` has been set to (`"Hello, World."`), and the text that was sent to the console (`"Hello, World.\n"`). Note the right pane discloses that the `print()` function added a newline (`\n`) character to the output.
- **4**: The output pane of the playground window shows the debug console, which in this case displays what the Swift program has output. If your code has errors, the debug console will output information about those errors as well.

Now that we have a development environment up and running where we can create and run Swift code, let's move on to learning about and using the Swift language.

Swift Variables and Constants

Virtually all programming languages include the ability for programmers to store values in memory using an associated name chosen by the programmer. Variables allow programs to operate on data values that change during the run of the program.

Declaring Swift Variables

A Swift variable declaration uses the following basic syntax:

```
var <variable name> : <type> = <value>
```

Given this syntax, a legal declaration for a Pi variable would be the following:

```
var pi : Double = 3.14159
```

This declaration means: *create a variable named* `pi`, *which stores a* `Double` *data type, and assign it an initial value of 3.14159.*

The Swift Standard Library has Pi built in, accessed by using the `Float.pi` and `Double.pi` properties.

Variables Versus Constants

You may want to store a named value in your program that will not change during the life of the program. In the previous example, the value of Pi should never change during the course of a program. How can we ensure that, once defined, this named value can never be accidentally changed by our code?

Swift *variables* are declared using the `var` keyword, while Swift *constants* are declared using the `let` keyword, for example:

```
var pi1 = 3.14159
let pi2 = 3.15159
```

In this code, the named value `pi1` is a variable, and its value can be changed by the code after it is declared. The following line of code later in the program would be legal, even though it would result in an invalid value for `pi1`:

```
pi1 = pi1 * 2.0
```

On the other hand, since `pi2` was declared as a constant, using the `let` keyword, the following line of code later in the program would result in a compile-time error, since changing a `let` constant is illegal:

```
pi2 = pi2 * 2.0
```

Generally, any time you create a named value that will never be changed during the run of your program, you should use the `let` keyword to create a constant. The Swift compiler enforces this recommendation by creating a compile-time warning whenever a `var` is created that is not subsequently changed.

 Other than the restriction on mutating the value of a constant once declared (for safety), Swift variables and constants are used in virtually identical ways, and you usually won't think about whether a symbol is a variable or a constant after declaring it.

Type Inference

In the previous example, we created the variable `pi1` without specifying its data type. We took advantage of a Swift compiler feature called **type inference**.

When you assign the value of a variable or constant as you create it, the Swift compiler will analyze the right-hand side of the assignment, *infer* the data type, and assign that data type to the variable or constant you're creating. For example, in the following declaration, the compiler will create the variable name as a String data type:

```
var name = "George Smith"
```

As a *type-safe* language, once a data type is inferred by the compiler, it remains fixed for the life of the variable or constant. Attempting to assign a non-string value to the name variable declared above would result in a compile-time error:

```
name = 3.14159  // Error: "Cannot assign value of type 'Double' to 'String'
```

While Swift is a *type-safe* language, where variable types are explicit and do not change, it is possible to create Swift code that behaves like a dynamic type language using the Swift Any data type. For example, the following code is legal in Swift:

```
var anyType: Any
anyType = "Hello, world"
anyType = 3.14159
```

While this is legal, it's not a good Swift programming practice. The Any type is mainly provided to allow bridging between Objective-C and Swift code. To keep your code as safe and error-free as possible, you should use explicit types wherever possible.

Variable Naming

Swift variables and constants have the same naming rules as most C-inspired programming languages:

- Must not start with a digit
- After the first character, digits are allowed
- Can begin with and include an underscore character
- Symbol names are case sensitive
- Reserved language keywords may be used as variable names if enclosed in backticks (for example, `` `Int` ``:Int = 5)

When creating variable and constant names in Swift, the generally accepted naming convention is to use a camelCase naming convention, beginning with a lowercase letter. Following generally accepted naming conventions makes code easier for others to read and understand (`https://swift.org/documentation/api-design-guidelines/#follow-case-conventions`).

For example, the following would be a conventional variable declaration:

```
var postalCode = "48108"
```

However, the following would not be conventional, and would be considered incorrect by many other Swift developers:

```
var PostalCode = "48108"
var postal_code  = "48108"
var POSTALCODE = "48108"
```

Unlike many other programming languages, Swift is not restricted to the Western alphabet for its variable name characters. You may use any Unicode character as part of your variable declarations. The following variable declarations are legal in Swift:

```
var helloWorld = "Hello, World"
var 你好世界 = "Hello World"
var ☺ = "Smile!"
```

> Just because you can use any Unicode character within a variable name, and can use reserved words as variables when enclosed in backticks, it doesn't mean you should. Always consider other developers who may need to read and maintain your code in the future. The priority for variable names is that they should make code easier to read, understand, and maintain.

Working with Variables

In this section, you'll use an Xcode playground to create a variable and constant, and observe the difference between them. So, let's get started.

To work with variables, follow these steps:

1. Launch Xcode as before, and create a new playground named `Create a Variable.playground`.

2. Add the following code to the playground to create a constant (that is, an immutable variable) named name, and a variable named address:

```
let name = "John Doe"
var address = "201 Main Street"
print("\(name) lives at \(address)")
```

In this code, both name and address store string text in named memory locations. And we can include them both in the print statement in the same way.

3. Now add the following code to change John Doe's address and print the new information to the console:

```
address = "301 Fifth Avenue"
print("\(name) lives at \(address)")
```

In the console output, the address is changed as expected.

4. Finally, let's try to change the string stored in the name variable:

```
name = "Richard Doe"
```

In this case, the Swift compiler generates a compile-time error:

```
Cannot assign to value: 'name' is a 'let' constant
```

By declaring name as an immutable variable with let, we let the compiler know no code should be allowed to change the content of the variable after its value is initially set.

Tuples

One of Swift's unique language features is its inclusion of **tuples**. By default, variables and constants store a single value. Tuples allow a variable or constant name to refer to a set of values. While tuples do not exist in many languages, you can think of them as *compound values,* and they function almost identically to a *structure,* which is a single named object which can store more than one variable embedded within it.

By using a tuple, we could take the following variable declaration:

```
var dialCode = 44
var isoCode = "GB"
var name = "United Kingdom"
```

We could combine it to the following:

```
var country = (44, "GB", "United Kingdom")
```

Then we can access the individual members of the tuple as follows:

```
print(country.0)   // outputs 44
print(country.1)   // outputs GB
print(country.2)   // outputs United Kingdom
```

Tuple members can also be given individual names, as follows:

```
var country = (dialCode: 44, isoCode: "GB", name: "Great Britain")

print(country.dialCode)   // outputs 44
print(country.0)                 // also outputs 44!
print(country.isoCode)    // outputs GB
print(country.name)         // outputs United Kingdom
```

Swift functions can accept multiple input parameters, but return only one value. A common use case for a tuple variable type is to include more than one value from a function:

```
func getCountry() -> (dialCode: Int, isoCode: String, name: String) {
    let country = (dialCode: 44, isoCode: "GB", name: "United Kingdom")
    return country
}

let ret = getCountry()

print(ret)
```

A second way to return multiple values from a function is to use `inout` parameters, which allows a function to change the value of an input parameter within that function.

While there are valid use cases for changing `inout` parameter values, returning a tuple has the advantage of returning a value type—rather than modifying input values.

 Tuples behave much like structures—which are predefined compound data types in Swift and many other languages. You may be tempted to use tuples rather than making the extra effort to create structures since they provide similar utility. Be careful not to overuse tuples. They are convenient for ad hoc, lightweight composite data types, but when used in complex programming, use cases can result in code that's more difficult to understand and harder to maintain. Use tuples as they're intended, as a means to bundle a few related components of a data element.

Creating a Tuple

Let's look at creating a tuple. We'll use an Xcode playground to create and use a tuple. Here are the steps:

1. Launch Xcode as before, and create a new playground named `Create a Tuple.playground`.

2. Add the following code to the playground to create a tuple containing a person's name, address and age:

```
let person1 = ("John Doe", "201 Main Street", 35)
print("\(person1.0) lives at \(person1.1) and is \(person1.2) years
old.")
```

This code is very similar to the previous , except that we've used a tuple to group together values describing John Doe — rather than using separate variables for each element.

While this syntax is legal, acceptable, and common, it can begin to result in difficult to understand and maintain code — especially when a tuple contains more than two simple values. To make a tuple more maintainable, you can give variable names to each of its components.

3. Add the following to the playground:

```
let person2 = (name: "Jane Doe", address: "301 Fifth Avenue", age: 35)
print("\(person2.name) lives at \(person2.address) and is \(person2.age)
years old.")
```

In this second approach, each member of the tuple has a descriptive name, making it easier for the reader of the program to understand and maintain the code.

Optionals

Another unique language feature Swift provides is the **optional**. In most programming languages, all variables and constants *must* hold some value. But, in the real world, sometimes a value is *unknown*. For example, an address may or may not contain a second address line, and more than 60 countries in the world don't use postal codes. Optionals allow variables to indicate whether their value is missing (that is, not assigned), or is truly a *blank value*.

When variables are declared optional in Swift, they behave very similarly to column values in SQL database such as Oracle, SQL Server, and MySQL.

Optionality for Swift variables is *optional* (pun intended). To declare a variable as an optional, add a question mark (?) to the end of its data type (or assign another optional variable's value to it so the optional property is inferred from the existing variable).

The following variable name *is not* an optional:

```
var name: String = "Hello"
```

This next variable name *is* an optional, and has an initial *value* of nil:

```
var name: String?
```

The presence of the question mark intuitively expresses that the variable may — or may not — contain a string. If the optional is not assigned a value, it will automatically be set to nil, meaning it has no value.

Declaring an Optional

Earlier in this lesson, we declared variables with initial values assigned. These variables are *not* optional, have a value, and can never be assigned a nil value, or an unwrapped optional variable's value.

In this section, we define a variable as an optional by adding a question mark to the type name, which makes it subject to the Swift compiler's optional validation rules.

A third possibility is to declare a **force unwrapped** variable — a variable that can be nil, but is not optional. This type of variable is declared by placing an exclamation point (!) after the type (rather than the question mark (?) for the optional), for example:

```
var customerAge: Int!
```

When a variable is declared in this fashion, the compiler *will* allow the variable to be assigned a nil value at any time, but *will not* warn the programmer at *compile time* when the variable's value is (or could be) assigned a nil value.

There are limited circumstances where this technique is required, and in general it should be avoided.

Why don't we make all variables optional? Optional is a powerful Swift feature, but working with optional variables requires more code as they are used, primarily to check for `nil` values before accessing the optional value. In general, you should use optional variables when variables may be missing values, but not use optional variables when you know a variable will always have a value.

Working with Optionals

As mentioned, the simplest way to declare a variable as an optional is to append the data type with a question mark, for example:

```
var name: String?
```

Because of Swift's type inference, the following line of code *will* create a second variable of optional type:

```
var nameCopy = name
```

The syntax to assign a value to this variable is the same as it would be if the variable was not declared as optional:

```
name = "Adam Smith"
```

The difference between optional and non-optional variables is primarily when you access the value of an optional, which we'll cover next.

Optional nil Values

Optional variables in Swift can be directly compared to the absence of value (`nil`) and assigned a `nil` value. For example, in the following two statements, variable a initially has a value of 4, then is assigned a `nil` value, and then is checked for having a `nil` value:

```
var a: Int? = 4
a = nil
if a == nil {
  print("a is nil")
}
```

While the presence or absence of a value within an optional can be directly tested, extracting and using the value contained within an optional requires that the optional (the envelope) be unwrapped, and the content (value) extracted. We'll learn how to do this next.

Accessing Optional Values

Think of an optional as a value *wrapped* in an envelope. You cannot access the contents of an envelope without opening it (*unwrapping* it), and then removing the contents.

You can primarily unwrap an optional and use its value in two ways:

- Force unwrap
- Conditional unwrap

We'll learn each of these techniques next.

Force Unwrapping an Optional

Look at the two optional Int variables:

```
var a: Int?
var b: Int = 4
```

You could attempt to assign a to b, for example:

```
b = a
```

But this would result in a compile-time error:

```
Value of optional type 'Int?' not unwrapped; did you mean to use '!' or
'?'?
```

As the error indicates, accessing the value of an unwrapped optional variable is (always) illegal. One approach to solving this problem is to force unwrap the variable as we use it. To force unwrap a variable, simply place an exclamation mark (!) after the variable name, for example:

```
b = a!
```

Force unwrapping is similar to using a **type cast** in many languages. In Swift, a force unwrap tells the compiler to assume that the optional contains a value.

However, a force unwrap shifts all the responsibility to the programmer for ensuring optionals actually have values. The above example, b = a!, would allow the code to compile, but would generate the following runtime error, and the application will crash:

```
Fatal error: Unexpectedly found nil while unwrapping an Optional value
```

Because variable a is an optional with no value, there is no value to extract from it to assign to b.

Force unwrapping should not be viewed as a way to *get around* compiler type-safety features. Only use force unwrapping when you're absolutely certain that it's impossible for an optional variable to contain a nil value. In the following code, a force unwrap would be acceptable:

```
var a: Int? = 2
var b: Int = 4
b = a!
```

Conditionally Unwrapping Optionals

While there are times when force unwrapping variables is safe, you should typically take advantage of Swift's type-safety features by using **conditional unwrapping**.

With conditional unwrapping, we ask the compiler to first check whether the optional has a value, and return the value if present, or nil if not.

For example, to assign the value of optional a to a new, non-optional variable b, we can use the following code:

```
var a: Int? = 4
if let b = a {
    print(b)
}
```

This code snippet would print the value 4 to the console. If we had not assigned the initial value 4 to a, then nothing would have been printed.

Using Optionals

Use an Xcode playground to create and use an optional, by performing the following steps:

1. Launch Xcode as before, and create a new playground named Using Optionals. playground.

2. Add the following code to the playground to create an optional containing a person's name:

   ```
   var name: String? = nil
   ```

3. Now add the following code to check whether the optional is nil:

   ```
   if name == nil {
       print("name is nil")
   } else {
   ```

```
    print("name is not nil")
}
```

Of course, since we assigned the value nil, it is nil.

A more common way to check for a non-nil optional is to use the if/let syntax covered previously.

4. Add the following code to assign a value to the optional content, then print it to the console:

```
name = "John Doe"
if let n = name {
    print(n)
} else {
print("the name is still nil")
```

Because you assigned a value to the variable name, the string John Doe is printed to the console.

5. Finally, comment out the variable assignment. The output will now change to the name is still nil, because the if/let syntax detected that the variable name contains no value.

The Swift guard Statement

It's very common that Swift functions should only execute when parameters passed to them are in an expected state. In early versions of Swift, the conditional unwrapping technique was often used to provide this type of safety checking. For example, a function that accepts an optional Int value, but should only proceed when the parameter is not nil might look as follows:

```
func doubleValue(input: Int?) -> Int? {
    if let i = input {
        return i * 2
    }
    return nil
}
```

While this function is only a few lines of code, imagine if the work done on the unwrapped variable was more complex. To allow parameter and other data state checking to be concisely done at the beginning of functions, Swift includes a guard keyword.

The following is a version of `doubleValue` that uses the `guard` syntax to place data state checks at the top of the function:

```
func doubleValue(input: Int?) -> Int? {
    guard let i = input else { return nil }
    return i * 2
}
```

This is the end of this section. Here, we have had a deep look at how to declare variables and constants in Swift. We also worked with tuples and optionals.

Activity: Variable Summary

In Swift, variables are declared before being used. Variables can be declared in various ways, and may not even need to have their type explicitly stated when the compiler can infer data type from initial assignment.

Use an Xcode playground to practice how to declare variables, constants, and tuples.

1. Launch Xcode as before, and create a new playground named `Topic B Summary.playground`.

2. Add the following code to the playground to create three variables storing values related to the weather conditions in Berlin:

    ```
    let cityName = "Berlin"
    var humidityPercentage: Double?
    var temperatureCentigrade: Double?
    ```

    Note that `cityName` is a constant, non-optional variable, with an initial string value. Since we know the name of the city in advance, and it doesn't change for this program, it's most appropriate to use `let` to declare this value as a constant.

    `humidityPercentage` and `temperatureCentigrade` are declared as optional, since we do not yet know the weather conditions in Berlin at the start of this program.

3. Next, add the following line of code to create a tuple to collect the weather report data into a single variable named `weather`:

    ```
    var weather = (city: cityName, humidityPercentage: humidityPercentage,
    temperature: temperatureCentigrade)
    ```

    Recall that providing reference names for each tuple member is optional, but is included here to make the remaining part of the program clearer to other programmers who may need to read this program later.

4. Next, set the value of humidity within the tuple:

```
weather.1 = 0.70
```

Note that even though you created a reference name for humidity (humidityPercentage), you can still set the value using the ordinal position within the tuple. The following line of code would probably be better in this case:

```
weather.humidityPercentage = 0.70
```

5. Now print the tuple to the console. On noticing that the variable provided is a tuple, the console print() function prints all members of the tuple — along with the reference names provided:

```
print(weather)
```

The output of the print statement is as follows:

```
(city: "Berlin", humidityPercentage: Optional(0.6999999999999996),
temperature: nil)
```

6. Finally, print each of the tuple's components, each on its own line:

```
print("City: \(weather.city)")
print("Humidity: \(String(describing:weather.humidityPercentage))")
print("Temperature: \(String(describing:weather.temperature))")
```

The output of this code is as follows:

```
City: Berlin
Humidity: Optional(0.6999999999999996)
Temperature: nil
```

Swift Data Types

Like most programming languages, Swift includes a full complement of built-in data types that store numbers, characters, strings, and Boolean values.

 In the previous section, we covered the use of Swift optionals, and worked through several examples declaring an Int variable as optional and non-optional. Keep in mind that any Swift variable, of any type, can be declared as an optional.

Numeric Data Types

Like most programming languages, Swift provides built-in numeric data types that represent either integer or floating-point values.

Int on 64-Bit Versus 32-Bit Platforms

While it's likely you'll develop Swift applications exclusively on 64-bit platforms, it's important to know that Swift is available on both 32-bit and 64-bit platforms. When using a generic integer numeric type (Int or UInt), the generic type will be mapped to an underlying, specific equivalent that matches the current platform's word size. For example, on a 64-bit platform, Int is mapped to Int64; on a 32-bit platform, the same Int type is mapped to an Int32.

Built-In Numeric Data Types

The following table summarizes the available Swift numeric data types:

Type	Min value	Max value
Int8	-128	127
Int16	-32768	32767
Int32	-2.1×10^9	2.1×10^9
Int64	-9.2×10^{18}	9.2×10^{18}
UInt8	0	255
UInt16	0	65535
UInt32	0	4.3×10^9
UInt64	0	1.8×10^{19}
Double	-1.8×10^{308}	1.8×10^{308}
Float	-3.4×10^{38}	3.4×10^{38}

Choosing the Appropriate Numeric Data Type

Conceptually, a UInt64 variable will consume four times more RAM than a UInt8 variable, so you may ask, "*Should I tune my variables by selecting the smallest number of bits needed to meet requirements?*"

While it may seem intuitive to select the numeric type that uses the least RAM to store the variable's expected range of values, it's usually preferable to use the generic integer types (for example, `Int` when declaring integers and `Double` when declaring floating-point numbers).

This is a reference from The Swift Programming Language (Swift 4): *"Unless you need to work with a specific size of integer, always use Int for integer values in your code. This aids code consistency and interoperability."* Visit `https://developer.apple.com/library/content/documentation/Swift/Conceptual/Swift_Programming_Language/` for the official documentation.

Declaring and Assigning Integer Variables

Integer values may be instantiated using base 10 (decimal), base 2 (binary), base 8 (octal), or base 16 (hexadecimal) literal values, or by assigning another `Int` variable of the same type to the new variable.

For example, assigning the number 100 to a new `Int` variable holding a duration in minutes can be done in any of the following ways:

```
let minutes = 100         // decimal
let minutes = 0b1100100   // binary
let minutes = 0o144       // octal
let minutes = 0x64        // hexadecimal
```

Declaring and Assigning Floating Point Numbers

Floating-point numbers are represented by either `Float` or `Double` data types. In general, you should use `Double` — and employ Float only when specific circumstances require using the smaller, 32-bit numeric variable.

Declaring and assigning value to floating-point variables follows the same syntax rules as with integer variables. For example, the following statement creates a new `Double` variable `interestRate`, and assigns an initial value to it:

```
var interestRate = 5.34
```

Numeric Literal Grouping

When assigning constant values to numeric types, Swift provides a handy format to make code more readable: the underscore character is ignored when parsing numeric literals.

This feature is most commonly used to provide *groupings of thousands* in a large integer or floating-point assignments, but actually can be used to provide any grouping separation that makes code more readable. For example, the following statements all assign the value 100,000 to the variable `minutes`:

```
var minutes = 100000
var minutes = 100_000
var minutes = 10_00_00
var minutes = 0b110_000110_101000_00
```

Using the underscore for readability can also be used for floating-point literal values. For example, the following statements are equivalent:

```
var balance = 10000.44556
var balance = 10_000.44_556
```

Numeric Type Conversions

Like many fully compiled languages, Swift is a *strongly typed* language, and requires explicit type conversions (or casts) when assigning the value from one variable type to a variable of a different type.

Many new Swift programmers find that Swift is even *stricter* than languages they've used before. In many programming languages, the compiler will implicitly convert between data types during an assignment so long as the value contained within the variable being assigned (on the right of the equals sign) could not overflow the variable being assigned to (on the left of the equals sign).

In other words, in many languages, the following code would be legal, since an `Int8` is known to always *fit* into an `Int16` without a numeric overflow:

```
Int8 smallNumber = 3;
Int16 mediumNumber = smallNumber;
```

However, this equivalent code in Swift would result in a compile-time error:

```
var smallNumber: Int8 = 3
var mediumNumber: Int16 = smallNumber
```

This code would generate the following error:

```
error: cannot convert value of type 'Int8' to specified type 'Int16'
```

In Swift, it's always the programmer's responsibility to ensure that assignments have the same data type on the left and right of the assignment operator (that is, the equals sign). The following code corrects the compile-time error:

```
var smallNumber: Int8 = 100
var mediumNumber: Int16 = Int16(smallNumber)
```

 This requirement for explicit type assignment is one reason why most Swift programming uses the generic numeric variables Int and Double, except when specific usage requires tuning for numeric range or memory storage size.

Using Numeric Types

Now, let's see how to use various numeric variable types by following these steps:

1. Launch Xcode as before, and create a new playground named `Topic B Using Numeric Types.playground`.

2. Add the following code to the playground to create three `Int` variables, using binary, base10, and base16 literal notation, respectively:

```
var base2 = 0b101010
var base10 = 42
var hex = 0x2A
```

3. Now add the following three corresponding lines to print the data type and value for each of the variables you just created.

```
print("Printing \(type(of: base2)): \(base2)")
print("Printing \(type(of: base10)): \(base10)")
print("Printing \(type(of: hex)): \(hex)")
```

Examining the output, note that the three variables all have the same data type (`Int`) and same value (42 in base 10).

4. Add the following lines of code to create two more variables, and to print the types and values for each:

```
var scientific = 4.2E+7
let double = 4.99993288828
print("Printing \(type(of: scientific)): \(scientific)")
print("Printing \(type(of: double)): \(double)")
```

Note that both variables were created as Double types—even though the value of the first is actually an Integer. Swift's inference system doesn't always look at the actual value. In this case, the presence of scientific notation in the literal value caused Swift to assume the value should be a Double.

5. Now add the following lines to *cast* and *round* the variable named `double` to an `Int`:

```
var castToInt = Int(double)
var roundToInt = Int(double.rounded())
print("Printing \(type(of: castToInt)): \(castToInt)")
print("Printing \(type(of: roundToInt)): \(roundToInt)")
```

As you probably expected, the `castToInt` discarded the fractional value of the original `double` variable. For the `roundToInt` variable, we called the `.rounded()` function on the variable `double`, and then cast that value. Since 4.999 was rounded up to 5 before being cast, the Int contains the rounded value.

6. Finally, add the following lines to create a very large unsigned integer and then print its type and value:

```
var bigUnsignedNumber:UInt64 = 18_000_000_000_000_000_000
print("Printing \(type(of: bigUnsignedNumber)): \(bigUnsignedNumber)")
```

This code works as expected—printing an integer with 20 digits (the underscore is added to help count how many digits there are).

Note that in this case, we specified `UInt64` should be the data type for this variable. Had we not made the type explicit, Swift's type inference rules would have assigned the smaller Int data type to the variable, and it would have overflowed.

Again, keep in mind the inference engine examines the format of a constant perhaps more than the value of the numeric value being assigned. You should rely on the inference engine by default, but keep in mind you may sometimes need to be explicit when you know more about how a variable will be used than Swift can infer.

Boolean

In Swift, the Boolean data type is Bool, and stores a value of `true` or `false`. As with other data types, in the case that a Bool value is not yet known, a Bool can be declared as optional, for example, `Bool?`.

For example, the following code declares a Boolean in Swift, and then changes its value:

```
var isChecked = false
isChecked = true
```

Testing for the value of a Bool value is similar to how we do it in other C-inspired languages, for example:

```
if isChecked {
    // statements to execute if isChecked is true
}
if isChecked == true {
    // statements to execute if isChecked is true
}
if !isChecked {
    // statements to execute if isChecked is false
}
```

Character

The Character data type in Swift is an *extended grapheme cluster*.

What does that mean?

An extended grapheme cluster is an ordered sequence of one or more Unicode scalars (that is, values) that, when taken together, produce a human-readable character.

Most important to understand is that, unlike ASCII or ANSI character representations many programmers have worked with before, a Character in Swift may be made of more than one Unicode value.

In Swift 4, the underlying complexities of Unicode, scalar values, and extended grapheme clusters are largely managed for you, but as you begin to work natively with Unicode characters and strings, bear in mind that the Swift Character/String architecture was developed from the ground up around Unicode character representation—not ANSI/ASCII as many other languages were.

Assigning a Character

The following are two examples creating new Character variables, and assigning literal values:

```
let ch1:Character = "A"
let ch2:Character = "😀"
```

Note the following regarding this assignment:

- In Swift, a Character literal is delimited by a double quote, rather than the single quote that's common in most C-inspired languages.

- Because the Swift compiler's type inference rules will assume double quotes around a literal imply a string variable, the above `ch1` assignment must explicitly declare the variables as Character type — otherwise the Swift compiler will create `ch1` as a string.

Constructing a Character Literal

To construct a Character type using Unicode values, you can assign an escape sequence, or use the UnicodeScalar struct to create a Character using numeric Unicode values as input.

The following line of code creates a UnicodeScalar from the value 65 (the ASCII value for the English letter A), and then assigns it to the immutable variable `ch1`:

```
let ch1 = Character(UnicodeScalar(65))
```

In this case, there is no ambiguity with regards to double quotation marks, so it's not necessary to explicitly assign the Character type during this assignment.

It's also common to construct a Character using a UnicodeScalar escape sequence within double quotation marks. The following creates a character variable containing an emoji character represented by the UnicodeScalar `1F601`:

```
let ch3 = "\u{1F601}"  // sets ch3 to "😁"
```

While Unicode scalars are conceptually similar to ASCII/ANSI value encoding, Swift Characters may be made of more than one numeric value, while ASCII and ANSI use only one numeric value to represent each character.

For example, an accented Western letter is expressed by providing a UnicodeScalar containing two character values.

We can construct the Unicode representation of an accented e character as follows:

```
let ch4 = "e\u{301}"    // é
```

The expression on the right of the assignment contains the literal letter e, followed by the escaped value for the accent modifier (301). The Swift compiler combines these two elements into a single extended grapheme cluster.

String

Strings in Swift are very similar to strings in other programming languages. As string handling is so central to any application development project, we'll dedicate an entire subsequent lesson to Swift's powerful string handling capabilities. In this section, we'll discuss the basics for declaring and using a string.

Fundamentally, strings are arrays of the Character types, supporting the familiar assignment operator (=), substrings, concatenation, and C-inspired escape characters.

Instantiating a String

Instantiating a string variable is highly intuitive. The following statements create string variables:

```
var alphabet = "ABCDEFGHIJKLMNOPQRSTUVWXYZ"
let macCharacters = "⌘^⌥⇧ ⌫⇪⌦→|"
let emoji = "😀😁😂😃😄😅😆😇"
```

String Concatenation

As in many languages, Swift strings can be concatenated using the plus (+) operator:

```
let alphaMac = alphabet + macCharacters
```

String also supports the unary addition operator:

```
alphabet += macCharacters
```

Extracting Characters

One difference between Swift strings and strings in many languages is how individual elements of strings are accessed. Specifically, the following syntax with Swift strings is illegal:

```
let ch = alphabet[4]
error: 'subscript' is unavailable: cannot subscript String with an Int, see
the documentation comment for discussion
```

In Swift, the input to the subscript operator (that is, what's between the [] characters) is expected to be of type `String.Index`, not `Int`.

In practice, you will construct an Index, then pass the index to the substring operator, for example:

```
let idx = alphabet.index(alphabet.startIndex, offsetBy: 4)
let ch = alphabet[idx]   // ch is assigned the character "E"
```

String Length

Obtaining the length of string is quite easy—simply call the `count` property of a string:

```
var alphabet = "ABCDEFGHIJKLMNOPQRSTUVWXYZ"
let alphabetLength = alphabet.count  // 26
```

We have now reached the end of this section. Here, we worked with the different data types in Swift, specifically numeric, Boolean, character, and string data types.

Activity: Data Type Summary

Now that you've learned about the various data types available with Swift, let's put this knowledge into practice by using various types together, and also using the Apple Foundation framework.

Use an Xcode playground to practice various data types. You'll be using numeric data types, formatting them as strings, and using string interpolation to print string values from various data types.

1. Launch Xcode as before, and create a new playground named `Data Type Summary.playground`.

2. Add the following code to the playground to create an immutable `Double` with an initial value:

   ```
   let dVal = 4.9876
   ```

3. Next, create a Boolean mutable variable with an initial value of `true`, and another variable set to the `Double` variable after rounding to a whole number:

```
var iValRounded = true
var iVal = Int(dVal.rounded())
```

4. Next, we're going to use a class from Foundation to create a string representation of the `Double` value, rounded to two digits. If you're not familiar with `NumberFormatter`, don't worry. This is just one of the many utility classes Apple provides in its expansive SDK for macOS and iOS:

```
var formatDigits = 2
let nf = NumberFormatter()
nf.numberStyle = .decimal
nf.maximumFractionDigits = formatDigits
let formattedDouble = nf.string(from: NSNumber(value: dVal)) ?? "#Err"
```

Because `NumberFormatter.string` returns an optional, we need either to check it (with `if`/`let`, or as here, provide a default value (`"#Err"`) in case the function does return `nil`.

5. Now add the following line to print a statement about the values we've created:

```
print("The original number was \(formattedDouble) (rounded to \
(formatDigits) decimal places), while the value \(iValRounded ?
"rounded" : "unrounded") to Integer is \(iVal).")
```

The output of this code is as follows:

```
The original number was 4.99 (rounded to 2 decimal places), while the
value rounded to Integer is 5.
```

6. Finally, add the following lines to change the rounding strategy, and print a sentence about the result of the new string conversions:

```
formatDigits = 0
nf.maximumFractionDigits = formatDigits
formattedDouble = nf.string(from: NSNumber(value: dVal)) ?? "#Err"
iValRounded = false
iVal = Int(dVal)
print("The original number was \(formattedDouble) (rounded to \
(formatDigits) decimal places), while the value \(iValRounded ?
"rounded" : "unrounded") to Integer is \(iVal).")
```

The output of this second sentence is as follows:

```
The original number was 5 (rounded to 0 decimal places), while the value
unrounded to Integer is 4.
```

Enums

Enums are frequently used in Swift to create custom data types that have a predefined set of possible values to select from. Enums serve to make code more readable and maintainable, and also provide compile-time checking for parameters and value assignments which yield higher quality, more robust code.

Many languages provide built-in enum features, and Swift's implementation of the enum is very similar to other languages. Swift does have some unique enum features, which we'll cover in this section.

Basic Enum Syntax

Consider the following code, which creates and uses a basic enum:

```
enum DayOfWeek {
    case monday, tuesday, wednesday, thursday, friday
}

var today = DayOfWeek.wednesday

if today == .friday {
    print("Today is Friday")
} else {
    print("Today is not Friday")
}
```

Defining the enum `DayOfWeek` declares a new data type, which can be used just like any other data type. Because the variable `today` is of the type `DayOfWeek`, which can only be assigned one of the seven listed values, we could not assign anything else. For example, the following code would generate a compile-time error, because `Saturday` is not included in the predefined values:

```
Var today = DayOfWeek.saturday
```

The preceding example illustrates the two most important advantages of enums:

- Possible values are restricted to a predefined list, making assignment of invalid values something that is tested at compile time rather than at runtime.
- Code that uses enums become self-documenting and easier to understand.

Enum with Raw Values

In the preceding enum example, the enum values (.monday, .tuesday, and so on) have no underlying data type. For example, we might want to calculate the *day of week* by subtracting the ordinal number for the today variable from .monday.

However, with the enum as defined, there is no numeric value associated, so the following code will fail to compile:

```
var nthDay = today - DayOfWeek.Monday
```

This code generates the following error:

```
Binary operator - cannot be applied to two 'DayOfWeek' operands
```

This is by design, because unlike some languages, a Swift enum need not be mapped to a native data type (and should not be, if there's no reason to do so).

However, Swift enums *can be* mapped to any underlying data type. In the following revision, we map the day of week to the Int data type, which enables the *nth day of the week* calculation mentioned above:

```
enum DayOfWeek: Int {
    case monday, tuesday, wednesday, thursday, friday
}

var today = DayOfWeek.Wednesday // DayOfWeek.wednesday
var nthDay = today.rawValue - DayOfWeek.monday.rawValue + 1 // 3
var tomorrow = DayOfWeek(rawValue: today.rawValue + 1) // DayOfWeek.
thursday
```

In this case, all we needed to do was add a native data type (Int) to the enum declaration. The Swift compiler then holds a .rawValue property. When an enum has an underlying value, it also becomes possible to create an enum member by passing it to the rawValue: parameter of the enum initializer.

 Use care with raw values. Passing a rawValue: to an enum initializer that does not match a defined case within the enum results in the creation of a nil optional.

In the preceding example, we used `Int` as the raw value for the revised `DayOfWeek` enum. Swift allows any data type to serve as the underlying value of an enum. For example, we could use String instead of `Int` to enable the following use case:

```swift
enum DayOfWeek: String {
    case monday = "Monday"
    case tuesday = "Tuesday"
    case wednesday = "Wednesday"
    case thursday = "Thursday"
    case friday = "Friday"
    case saturday = "Saturday"
}


var today = DayOfWeek.Wednesday // DayOfWeek.wednesday
let dayString = today.rawValue  // "Wednesday"
```

In this section, we have looked at enums in detail. We saw its syntax and how to define an enum with raw values. We will now work through an activity where we will use enums to implement error codes.

Activity: Using Swift Enums

Enumerations are a powerful construct available in many programming languages. Enumerations make code more robust and easier for others to understand and maintain.

Use Xcode to define error codes using conventional *error number* techniques, and alternatives that use Swift enums.

1. Launch Xcode as before, and create a new playground named `Activity D - Using Numeric Types.playground`.

2. Add the following lines of code to create a set of error codes using simple integer values:

```swift
// Store an error condition as an integer
let success = 0
let ioFailure = 1
let timeoutFailure = 2
```

3. Now create the same set of error codes using an enum *without* a raw value:

```
// Store an error condition as an enum type
enum Result {
    case success
    case ioFailure
    case timeoutFailure
}
```

4. Finally, create the same set again, this time using an enum *with* a raw Integer value associated with each result code:

```
// Store an error condition as an enum type with raw value
enum ResultWithRawValue: Int {
    case success = 0
    case ioFailure = 1
    case timeoutFailure = 2
}
```

5. Now let's use these error values by creating a new variable, assigning the ioFailure error condition to each one:

```
let error1 = ioFailure
let error2 = Result.ioFailure
let error3 = ResultWithRawValue.ioFailure
```

6. Finally, use the console print function to output the content of each error variable. Note how each one is represented to the console:

```
// Now print out the error result from each case.
print("File access resulted: \(error1)")
print("File access resulted: \(error2)")
print("File access resulted: \(error3)")
print("File access resulted: \(error3.rawValue)")
```

Summary

In this lesson, we've learned the basic language structure and syntax for the Swift programming language. We've now understood the following concepts:

- The fundamental structure of Swift programs, and how to use an Xcode playground to develop simple and complex programs
- How to create and use mutable and immutable Swift variables
- The built-in data types available to Swift programs, and how to select the appropriate data type depending on circumstance
- Swift's powerful optional construct for detecting and branching program flow when data values are not available
- Swift's type inference and strict type safety syntax and usage

Now that you have the basics well in hand, we're ready to move on to the next lesson, where we'll learn how to use these language elements in complex Swift programs. Specifically, we'll look at the control flow structures and operators offered by Swift.

2
Swift Operators and Control Flow

In the last lesson, you learned the fundamentals of Swift syntax, data types, and how to use variables to store and operate on data in a Swift program.

In this lesson, you'll learn how to use the fundamental flow control structures and language elements that form the building blocks for Swift programs.

Swift contains a full set of flow control constructions that help you build logic and organize applications. Swift implements control structures you'll find familiar, and Swift adds modern features and extensions not available in some other languages.

This lesson also covers the broad range of Swift logical and bitwise operators. Swift supports a comprehensive set of operators, based on the C operator construction—but with modern extensions that we'll fully cover in this lesson.

Lesson objectives

By the end of this lesson, you will be able to do the following:

- Use the assignment, arithmetic, and bitwise operators
- Use Swift's comparison operators
- Explain the functionality of Swift's range operators
- Use the Swift branching features: `if` and `switch`
- Control program flow with loops, such as `for`, `while`, and `repeat/while`

Swift Operators

Operators are special characters—usually drawn from mathematics—that are used to process evaluations, modify variable values, and combine values. Swift operators break down into categories by the function they perform:

- Assignment operators
- Arithmetic operators
- Comparison operators
- Logical operators
- Bitwise operators
- Nil-coalescing operators
- Range operators

Refer to the following diagram:

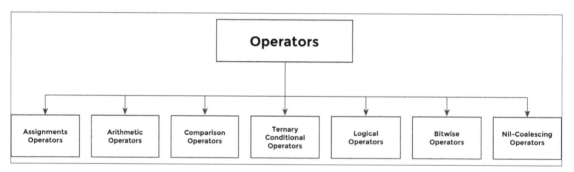

Swift implements its assignment, arithmetic, comparison, logical, and bitwise operators nearly identically to other C-inspired languages, such as C++, Java, and C#—so your previous experience with these operators will apply directly to Swift programming.

In this lesson, we'll summarize this common set of operators, and only highlight unique Swift implementations. Should you need detailed information on the meaning of any of these operators, please refer to Apple's *The Swift Programming Language* guide (`https://developer.apple.com/library/content/documentation/Swift/Conceptual/Swift_Programming_Language/`).

The `nil` coalescing and range operators are unique to Swift and you may not have encountered them before—we'll cover these operators in detail.

Assignment Operator

Swift uses the equals sign (=) to assign the value of one object to another, for example:

```
let x = 3.0
```

Like most languages, the equals sign is not overloaded for comparison. Thus, the following is not a valid `if` statement:

```
if x = 3 {
    // do something
}
// error: use of '=' in a boolean context, did you mean '=='?
```

Arithmetic Operators

Let's look at the arithmetic operators, beginning with the standard ones.

Standard Arithmetic Operators

Swift supports the four standard arithmetic operators for number types:

Addition	+
Subtraction	-
Multiplication	*
Division	/

Remainder Operator

Swift's remainder operator (%) returns the remainder when a second operand is divided into a first operand. For example, the result (r) in the following expression is 2, since 14/4=3, with a remainder of 2:

```
let r = 14 % 4    // r == 2
```

 The remainder operator (%) is designed to accept Int operands. To calculate the remainder for floating-point numbers, instead use the function remainder(dividingBy:), for example:

```
let r = 15.3.remainder(dividingBy: 5.0) // r == 0.3
```

Unary minus Operator

Use the unary minus operator (-) before a variable or constant to return the value multiplied by -1, for example:

```
let x = 3    // x == 3
let y = -x   // y == -3
```

Compound Assignment Operators

Swift supports the compound assignment operators as a shortcut for assigning a variable the value of itself changed with another numerical operator. For example, the following two statements are equivalent:

```
x = x + 1
x += 1
```

Unlike C (and some C-inspired languages), Swift does not support the use of the ++ unary operator. The following is *not* a Swift syntax:

```
x++     // Unary operator '++' cannot be applied
```

Comparison Operators

Swift's comparison operators are nearly identical to other C-inspired languages. We'll summarize them and any key differences in this section.

Equality

To compare whether the value of two value types are equal (for example, whether two `Int` variables contain the same value), use the double-equals sign, for example:

```
if x == 3 {
    // do something
}
```

To compare whether two class instances are the same instance, use the triple-equals sign, for example:

```
if obj1 === obj2 {
  // do something if the variables refer to the same object
}
```

Inequality

To test for inequality (rather than equality), replace the first equals sign with an exclamation point:

Test for equality	Test for inequality
==	!=
===	!==

Comparison between Two Values

Swift inequality operators are straightforward, each returning a Bool type. The following table explains each one:

Greater than	>
Less than	<
Greater than or equal to	>=
Less than or equal to	<=

Ternary Conditional Operator

This operator provides a shorthand for assignments to variables that result from *if…then… else* structured comparisons. For example, the following two statements are equivalent:

```
// conventional if..then..else
if x > 4 {
    y = 1
} else {
    y = 2
}
// ternary conditional operator
y = x > 4 ? 1 : 2
```

Logical Operators

Swift's logical operators follow the same conventions as other C-inspired languages. The following logical operators are available:

NOT	!
AND	&&
OR	||

Local operators can be chained in a single expression, for example:

```
let canEnter = atDoor && doorUnlocked || haveKey
```

Local operators are evaluated as a chain of pairs, and are left associative, meaning that this expression is evaluated as follows:

```
let canEnter = (atDoor && doorUnlocked) || haveKey
```

This statement as written suggests a visitor should have a key whether the door is locked or unlocked — which is probably not what was intended. Change the order of evaluation for logical operators using parentheses to get what we want:

```
let canEnter = atDoor && (doorUnlocked || haveKey)
```

Bitwise Operators

Swift's bitwise operators also follow the same conventions as other C-inspired languages. The following bitwise operators are available:

NOT	~
AND	&
OR	|
XOR	^
Left shift	<<
Right shift	>>

Nil-Coalescing Operator

The nil-coalescing operator is used when unwrapping an optional when a default value is desired in the case that the optional is nil.

The following code unwraps an optional with and without nil-coalescing:

```
let x:Int?
let y = x        // y is an optional of type Int?, and is nil
let z = x ?? 4   // z is a non-optional Int, with value 4
```

Range Operators

Swift range operators are unique, and many developers new to Swift have not encountered this type of operator in other languages. Range operators are used to express a range of values in a concise syntax.

We will use a range operator when we will introduce the for loop:

```
for var i in 0..<10 {
    print(i)
}
```

The for loop iterates over a range of Int values (1,2,3,4,5,6,7,8,9,10), which are created using the range operator . .<.

Range operators can be classified into three types:

- Closed range operator
- Half-open range operator
- One-sided range operator

Closed Range Operator

To create a range that includes the beginning and ending elements, use the closed range operator, which is indicated by three periods (. . .):

```
let numbers = 0...10    // numbers = [0,1,2,3,4,5,6,7,8,9,10]
```

Half-Open Range Operator

The half-open range operator (. .<) creates a range that includes the first specified element and all values before the ending element:

```
let numbers = 0..<10    // numbers = [0,1,2,3,4,5,6,7,8,9]
```

One-Sided Range Operator

One-sided range operators are variations on the closed and half-open operators. As the name suggests, the one-sided variants exclude one of the bounding elements, creating a range that includes all possible values on the unbounded side of the operator:

```
let a = [-1,-2,-3,0,1,2,3]
let b = a[2...]        // b = [-3,0,1,2,3]
let c = a[...2]        // c = [-1,-2,-3]
let e = a[..<2]        // d = [-1,-2]
```

Here, 2 refers to the position of a value in the array.

This is the end of this section. We have covered the various operators available in Swift in detail.

Activity: Operators

Swift provides a rich set of operators you can use to manipulate and transform data within your program. Many of the Swift operators will be familiar, while some provide powerful modern features you may not be familiar with.

Use an Xcode playground to practice using Swift operators.

1. Launch Xcode, create a new playground, and save it to your desktop with the name `Operators.playground`.

2. Add a custom class called `MyString`, which contains a single string object. Don't worry that we haven't formally covered objects — we'll be covering them fully in the next lesson! For now, know that a class is a custom type you can create that contains variables and methods:

```
class MyString {
    var content = "Foo"
}
```

3. Next, create two instances of your custom class: `string1`, `string2`, and a constant `string3` assigned the value `string2`:

```
let string1 = MyString()
let string2 = MyString()
let string3 = string2
```

4. Use variables to evaluate whether the content and instances are equal to each other:

```
var isContentEqual = string1.content == string2.content
var isObjectEqual = string1 === string2
isObjectEqual = string2 === string3
```

5. Change the content of one of the strings, and re-evaluate whether the content and object equality has changed:

```
string2.content = "Bar"
isContentEqual = string1.content == string2.content
isObjectEqual = string1 === string2
```

6. Finally, use a `for` loop with a bitwise operator to print `Int` values containing only one on bit (we'll cover `for` loops in detail in the next section):

```
let val = 1

for i in 1..<16 {
    print("\(val) shifted left \(i) times is \(val << i)")
}
```

Branching

Flow control structures enable developers to apply logical processes and make decisions about what code is executed. Most modern programming languages provide a similar set of flow control structures:

- The `if` statements execute code blocks when a Boolean condition is `true`.
- The `while` loops execute blocks of code while a Boolean condition remains `true`.
- The `for` loops execute blocks of code a specific number of times.

It's said that virtually any programming control flow requirement can be implemented with a `while` statement alone. However, the other various control structures allow programmers to create control flow that's more concise and clearly expresses the intent of the logical program flow.

Indeed, Swift provides a rich and powerful set of control structures, which you'll learn about in this section.

The if Statement

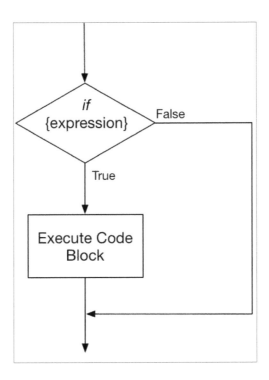

The most basic flow control statement in programming is the if statement, which executes a block of code *if* some Boolean expression is true. The preceding diagram is the flow chart of the if statement. The syntax for the Swift if statement is as follows:

```
if {condition-list} {
    {statements}
} else {
    {statements}
}
```

The following code example implements an if statement:

```
Let age = 18
if age >= 18 {
    print("person can vote")
}
```

A *{condition-list}* can be one or more expressions that each return a Bool data type. Any of the following are valid for a Swift *{condition}*:

- A variable of Bool type
- Use of a comparison operator which returns a Bool type (for example, ==, >, >=, and so on)
- The Bool constants `true` and `false`
- Calling a function that returns a Bool data type

Swift has several rules regarding the `if` statement that may be different from other programming languages you're familiar with:

- Parentheses aren't added around the *{boolean expression}*, as they are in most C-inspired languages
- The *{statements}* must be enclosed in curly braces — even if there is only a single statement.
- Swift allows multiple *{conditions}* in a comma-separated list. All conditions in the condition list must be satisfied for the code block to be executed.

Condition Lists

The Swift `if` statement can accept multiple, independent *{condition}* clauses, in a comma-delimited fashion.

In the following code sample, the code block is executed only when the `isCar` and `isNew` values are both true:

```
let isCar = true
let isNew = true

if isCar, isNew {
    print("new car")
}
```

Swift also supports the use of logical operators when writing the condition portion of an if statement. For example, in the previous code, the following would be the equivalent in Swift:

```
if isCar && isNew {
    print('new car")
}
```

However, condition lists are required when using the if statement to unwrap optional values as part of a condition, which you'll learn about in the next section.

Optional Unwrapping with if

You'll use the if statement to unwrap optional values frequently. In fact, the if construction will probably be the most frequent way you'll access values stored in optionals!

We covered optionals in the previous lesson.

Unwrapping a variable with the if statement is done by embedding an assignment into a new variable within the if statement condition list, for example:

```
let price:Double? = 5.99
if let p = price, p > 5.0 {
    print(p)
}
```

In this case, the original variable, price, is an optional. In the first clause of the condition list, we ask the compiler to check for a value within the optional price, and if there is one, assign it to the new constant p. Then, the second clause of the condition list tests whether the unwrapped value is greater than 5.0, and if so, the code block is executed.

If the optional price had been nil, the comparison clause would not have been executed, and the code block would not have executed. Program flow would have continued after the if block.

Incidentally, when using the if statement to unwrap a variable, it can be unwrapped into a mutable variable if required. For example, the following code sample extracts the optional value into the variable p, which is then modified before the print statement:

```
let price:Double? = 5.99
if var p = price {
    p += 1
    print(p)
}
```

The switch Statement

Have a look at the following diagram. It illustrates how the switch statement works:

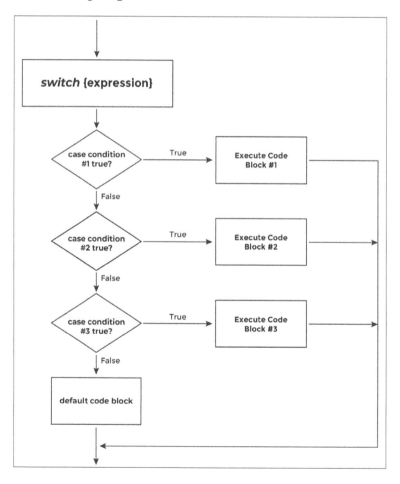

A switch statement is a powerful and flexible branching structure that most developers will use very often in their programs. Swift's switch has powerful, flexible features that we'll cover in detail next.

Creating a program that needs to execute different code blocks depending on the same *{Boolean expression}* is a common requirement, and can be implemented with the if statement as follows:

```
if personAge < 1 {
    print("baby")
} else if personAge < 3 {
    print("toddler")
} else if personAge < 5 {
    print("preschooler")
} else if personAge < 13 {
    print("gradeschooler")
} else if personAge < 18 {
    print("teen")
} else {
    print("adult")
}
```

The preceding code implements the requirement to print a child's life stage depending on their current age, but repeating the condition for each case quickly becomes repetitive and can be more prone to coding errors than a more concise switch statement.

The previous code fragment can be easily rewritten with a switch/case statement as follows:

```
switch personAge {
    case 0..<1: print("baby")
    case 1..<3: print("toddler")
    case 3..<5: print("preschooler")
    case 5..<13: print("gradeschooler")
    case 13..<18: print("teen")
    default: print("adult")
}
```

A switch statement evaluates a single control expression, personAge, in this case, and then executes the lines of code contained within the first matching case block.

Using the switch control structure to implement this logic results in code that's more concise and easier to read and maintain.

switch Statement Rules

There are a few syntax rules to note when using the Swift `switch` statement:

- The cases within a `switch` statement must be exhaustive. In the example above, the special default case is included to mean *"When no other case is matched, do this...."*

- If a default case is included, it must be the last case before the `switch` statement's closing brace.

- If the `switch` statement's control expression matches more than one case expression, Swift will execute only the statements included with the first matching case.

- A case must include at least one line of code. If you don't intend to execute any code when a case is matched, add a single `break` keyword to inform the compiler you intend for no code to be executed when the case is true.

- By default, Swift's `switch` statement does not support fallthrough to code in other cases. Fallthrough is supported via the `fallthrough` keyword.

The `switch` statement goes much further, and has many powerful extensions, which we'll review next.

The break Keyword

As mentioned above, if a case is matched that should run no code, simply include a `break` statement.

The following example will print baby for ages < 1, `adult` for ages > 17, and print nothing for ages 1-17:

```
switch personAge {
    case 0..<1: print("baby")
    case 1..<18: break
    default: print("adult")
}
```

The fallthrough Keyword

If a matched case should execute statements declared for the case that directly follows it, use the `fallthrough` keyword.

The following example will group all school age (ages 3-17) people with the `teen` category:

```
switch personAge {
    case 0..<1: print("baby")
    case 1..<3: print("toddler")
    case 3..<5: fallthrough
    case 5..<13: fallthrough
    case 13..<18: print("teen")
    default: print("adult")
}
```

Matching Non-Scalar Values

Unlike many other programming languages, Swift *does not* limit `switch` statements to scalar data types. The expression provided to a `switch` statement can be a variable holding a scalar (discrete) set of values — as the previous examples have been — but can also be floating-point, string, enumerations, or any type for which you can write a valid matching expression for each case pattern.

The following example is a valid `switch` statement using a `Double` data type as input:

```
switch temperature {
    case -29.0..<(-7.0): print("bitter cold")
    case -7.0..<12.0: print("cold")
    case 12.0..<20: print("warm")
    case 20..<40.0: print("hot")
    default: print("deadly")
}
```

Switch can also be used to match non-numeric values, such as String values:

```
let quarterName = "Second Quarter"
var quarterNum: Int?

switch quarterName {
    case "First Quarter": quarterNum = 1
    case "Second Quarter": quarterNum = 2
    case "Third Quarter": quarterNum = 3
    default: quarterNum = 4
}
```

Multiple Patterns in a Single Case

A single case within a `switch` statement can match multiple patterns, as shown here:

```
let monthName = "February"
var quarterNum: Int?

switch monthName {
   case "January", "February", "March": quarterNum = 1
   case "April", "May", "June": quarterNum = 2
   case "July", "August", "September": quarterNum = 3
   default: quarterNum = 4
}
```

Using the where Statement within case

Swift provides the flexibility to add evaluation logic within a `case` statement. This flexibility allows a case to be matched only when specific conditions are true.

The following `switch` statement branches on the relationship between two variables, `temperature` and `humidity`:

```
let temperature = 21.5
let humidity = 22.0

switch (temperature, humidity) {
   case let (t,h) where t > h: print("humidity lower")
   case let (t,h) where t < h: print("humidity higher")
   default: "humidity and temperature are the same"
}
```

Swift allows the flexibility for cases to use where in some case expressions but not in others, for example:

```
let responseCode = 501

switch(responseCode) {
    case 200: print("ok")
    case let code where code >= 500: print("server error")
    default: print("Request failed for another reason")
}
```

Evaluating Optionals with a switch Statement

The switch statement can branch depending on whether a Swift optional is nil, and then evaluate the value contained in a non-nil optional:

```
let responseCode:Int?
let error:Error?
// make a web service call, which will set responseCode or error to non-nil
switch (error, responseCode) {
    case (.none, .some(let code)) where code == 200: print("success")
    case (.some(let err), .none): print(err.localizedDescription)
    default: print("something else happened")
}
```

As you can see already, the switch statement in Swift is highly flexible and can meet a vast array of use cases! In general, whenever you include multiple code branches based on the value of a single variable (or related set of variables), consider using the switch statement rather than constructing a series of nested if/else statements.

Activity: Converting Code from if to switch

The switch statement is essentially a more structured and readable way to implement a nested if statement. It's common to refactor a nested if to a case statement to make the code more readable and maintainable. Let's do this now.

Use an Xcode playground to convert a code with if statements to an equivalent code with switch statements.

1. Launch Xcode, create a new playground, and save it to your desktop with the name CaseRefactor.playground.

2. Add the following code, which uses a nested if statement to determine the country code given a country name:

```
let countryName = "United States"
var countryCode = ""

if countryName == "United Kingdom" {
    countryCode = "GB"
} else if countryName == "Mexico" {
    countryCode = "MX"
} else if countryName == "Canada" {
    countryCode = "CA"
} else if countryName == "Spain" {
    countryCode = "ES"
} else if countryName == "United States" {
    countryCode = "US"
} else {
    countryCode = "??"
}
print("Country named '\(countryName)' has code \(countryCode)")
```

3. Next, let's employ an enumeration, which we learned in the last lesson, to encapsulate the country names into a more maintainable data structure. Add the following code underneath the print statement:

```
enum Countries:String {
    case uk = "United Kingdom"
    case mx = "Mexico"
    case ca = "Canada"
    case es = "Spain"
    case us = "United States"
```

```
        case unknown = ""
}
```

4. Add a `switch` statement, which accomplishes the same logic as the nested `if` — but in a more readable and structured way. Also note that because a `case` statement is required to be exhaustive, it would be a compiler error to forget to add countries included in the enumeration to the `case` statement:

```
switch Countries(rawValue: countryName) ?? .unknown {
    case .uk: countryCode = "GB"
    case .mx: countryCode = "MX"
    case .ca: countryCode = "CA"
    case .es: countryCode = "ES"
    case .us: countryCode = "US"
    case .unknown: countryCode = "??"
}
```

5. To make the conversion complete, add the original `print` statement below the `switch` statement:

```
print("Country named '\(countryName)' has code \(countryCode)")
```

Loops

After the branching structures `if` and `switch`, the most common structures you'll use in your programming are looping structures, which cause your program flow to execute the same code iteratively.

The looping structures you'll learn in this section are the following:

- `for...in`, which executes the same code a predetermined number of times
- `while` and `repeat...while`, which executes code until a `true` condition becomes `false`

As with the `switch` control structure, there are many features and flexible options provided by these structures that make Swift more expressive and powerful than many other programming languages.

The for...in Statement

The following diagram illustrates how the for...in statement works:

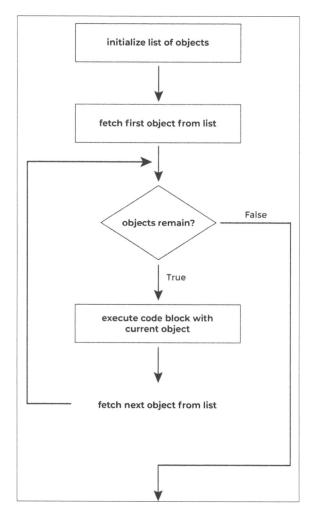

Most programming languages have a for statement used to execute a code statement a certain number of times. The preceding diagram illustrates how the for...in statement works. A canonical example of a for loop in C, similar to many other C-inspired languages, is the following:

```
for(int i=0; i<10; i++)
    printf("i=%d\n", i);
```

The equivalent `for` loop written in Swift is as follows:

```
for var i in 0..<10 {
    print(i)
}
```

Comparing the two `for` loops, they appear quite similar, but you could argue the Swift version is easier to read!

In Swift, a `for...in` loop always iterates over a collection of values, rather than simply serving as a mechanism to count iterations. The range operator used in the preceding example returns a set of `Int` values, which are then iterated over.

Internally, Swift creates an Iterator, then calls the `next()` method of the Iterator until `next()` returns `nil`, running the code block for each iteration.

Iterating over Objects

Although the previous code example actually does iterate over `Int` values, it's effectively running a code block a specific number of times. More often, you'll use `for...in` to iterate over a collection of objects stored in your application.

The most common method to iterate over a set of objects is to use the `for` syntax, as in the following example:

```
let strings = ["First String", "Second String", "Third String", "Fourth
String"]
for obj in strings {
    print(obj)
}
```

Using this syntax, the `print` statement within the block is executed once for each object in the `strings` array. Swift implicitly creates the constant variable `obj` for use within the block.

In the previous example, the `obj` local variable is implicitly created as a constant (that is, `let`).

While `let` is the default behavior, you can instruct the `for` loop to create a mutable variable by specifying `var` in the `for` loop declaration, as follows:

```
for var obj in strings {
    obj = "obj is: \(obj)"
    print(obj)
}
```

Iterating over Array Objects with index

The preceding example iterates over the `strings` array, providing each string to the execution block in a local variable named `obj`. Sometimes, the code may need to know the ordinal position of the object being processed. This can be accomplished by using the Array `enumerated` member function of the collection being iterated:

```
for (index, text) in strings.enumerated() {
    print("The object at index \(index) is \(text)")
}
```

The for Loop where Clause

The next feature of the `for` loop we'll learn is using the `where` clause to control which iterations are processed.

In the previous examples, the code always outputs all of the strings in the variable `strings`. We might want to only output strings meeting a certain test, for example, only strings beginning with the letter `F`:

One way to accomplish this requirement would be to rewrite the `for` loop as follows:

```
let strings = ["First String", "Second String", "Third String", "Fourth String"]

for string in strings {
    if string.starts(with: "F") {
        print(string)
    }
}
```

An even more concise way to write this code is to use the `for` loop's `where` clause, as follows:

```
let strings = ["First String", "Second String", "Third String", "Fourth
String"]

for string in strings where string.starts(with: "F") {
    print(string)
}
```

The break Control Transfer Statement

Like most C-inspired languages, Swift supports the use of the `break` control transfer statement in `for` loops.

The `break` statement has the effect of immediately transferring program flow to the statement following the `for` loop, effectively skipping the remaining portion of the current iteration, and cancelling all remaining iterations.

In the following example, the code within the `for` loop tests whether the current iteration's string begins with the letter T. If so, the `for` loop is immediately exited:

```
let strings = ["First String", "Second String", "Third String", "Fourth
String"]

for string in strings {
    if string.starts(with: "T") {
        break
    }
    print(string)
}
```

The continue Control Transfer Statement

Swift also supports the use of the `continue` control transfer statement in `for` loops.

The `continue` statement has the effect of skipping the remaining portion of the current iteration. Control then passes to the *top* of the `for` loop, where the next iteration proceeds (if there is a next iteration available).

In the following example, the `continue` control transfer statement is used to skip any iteration having a string starting with the letter F:

```
let strings = ["First String", "Second String", "Third String", "Fourth
String"]

for string in strings {
    if string.starts(with: "F") {
        continue
    }
    print(string)
}
```

Swift provides a simple, expressive, and powerful `for` loop for you to use in your programs. Key points to keep in mind regarding usage of the `for` loop are as follows:

- `for` always iterates over a collection of elements (and is not simply a counting variation of the `while` loop as it is in some programming languages).

- The Swift Standard Library includes many functional programming methods that can generate transformed object collections (for example `enumerated()` as we did above). Use these methods to maintain simpler logic within your loops.

- `for` loops support the `break` and `continue` control transfer statements to provide flow control exceptions controlled by the code block they iterate over.

The while Loop

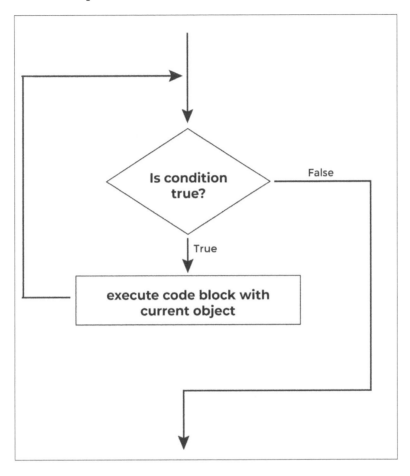

Where the `for` loop executes a code block a predetermined number of times, the `while` loop continues executing a code block until a Boolean expression evaluates as `false`. The preceding diagram illustrates how the while loop works.

The general syntax of the `while` loop is as follows:

```
while {condition-list} {
    statements
}
```

The syntax rules for the `while` loop are essentially identical to that of the `if` statement, specifically the following ones:

- *{condition-list}* can be one or more conditions, each returning a Boolean value
- *{condition-list}* can include the unwrapping of an optional value, which is then used in the code block
- There are no parentheses around the *{condition-list}*
- The code block must be enclosed in curly braces

The `while` statement supports the `break` and `continue` keywords to redirect flow control in the same manner as the `for` loop.

The following example uses a `while` loop to iterate over an array of `Double` values to calculate an average for all prices less than seven (7):

```
let price: [Double] =
    [1.99, 2.99, 3.99, 4.99, 5.99, 6.99, 7.99, 8.99]
var total = 0.0
var i = 0
while i < price.count && price[i] < 7.0 {
    i += 1
    total += price[i]
}
print(total / Double(i))  // 5.49
```

The repeat...while Loop

Because it evaluates its condition(s) prior to the first iteration, a `while` loop occasionally won't meet your needs. If you won't know whether a `while` loop should continue until after the first iteration, use the `repeat...while` variant.

If you were developing a console application that should play a game until the user pressed *Enter* without entering text, a `repeat...while` loop would be the ideal solution. For example, the following Swift command-line program effectively uses `repeat...while` where a `while` loop would be awkward:

```
#!/usr/bin/swift

func playGame() {
    print("simulate gameplay")
}

repeat {
```

```
    playGame()
    print("enter q to quit")
} while readLine() != "q"
```

 In most other programming languages, the Swift `repeat...while` statement is called `do...while`. In Swift 1.0, this statement did use the more traditional `do...while` name. However, when Swift added exception handling, the `do` keyword was given to that feature, and replaced with the keyword `repeat`.

This completes our look at the loops. Loops in Swift are important to implement the various program flow structures you might need to develop a variety of custom applications.

Activity: Implementing Loops

Loops and iteration are a core part of any computer program. Data is often stored in array and collection data structures, and loops allow you to develop concise, well-organized code to operate on them.

Use an Xcode playground to practice using the looping flow control structures we have covered in this section.

1. Launch Xcode and create a new playground, then save it to your desktop with the name Loops.playground.

2. Add the following declaration of a new array, which contains a list of Canadian provinces:

```
let provinces = ["Ontario", "Quebec", "Nova Scotia",
              "New Brunswick", "Manitoba",
              "British Columbia", "Prince Edward Island",
              "Saskatchewan", "Alberta",
              "Newfoundland and Labrador" ]
```

3. Add the following `repeat...while` loop to print each of the provinces to the console:

```
var i = 0
repeat {
    print(provinces[i])
    i += 1
} while i < provinces.count-1
print("===============")
```

4. Add the following `while` loop to print the same list of provinces to the console:

```swift
i = 0
while i < provinces.count-1 {
    print(provinces[i])
    i += 1
}
print("==============")
```

5. Add the following `for` loop to build a string containing the first letters of all provinces, and then print to the console as a sorted unique set of letters:

```swift
var firstLetters = ""

for province in provinces {
    firstLetters += province.prefix(1)
}
print("Canadian provinces start with one of the following letters: \
(Set(firstLetters).sorted())")
```

6. Finally, use a `for` loop with `enumerated` to determine the array indices of all provinces starting with the letter N:

```swift
var nProvinces = [Int]()
for (index, province) in provinces.enumerated() {
    if province.prefix(1) == "N" {
        nProvinces.append(index)
    }
}
print("The indices of provinces starting with 'N' are: \(nProvinces)")
```

Summary

In this lesson, you've learned how to use Swift's key language:

- Assignment, arithmetic, and bitwise operators
- Comparison and range operators
- The Swift branching features: `if` and `switch`
- Loops: `for`, `while`, `repeat...while`

You now have the skills needed to develop robust applications using Swift's powerful and expressive language syntax. In the next lesson, you'll learn the skills to develop functions and classes to organize your code. You will also explore and use error handling to efficiently handle unexpected errors in your programs.

3

Functions, Classes, and Structs

In the previous two lessons, you learned the fundamentals of Swift syntax, data types, and how to use variables to store data in a Swift program. With knowledge of these language elements, you're already prepared to create fully functional Swift programs.

In this lesson, you'll build on these skills, and learn how to develop fully featured Swift applications, catch unexpected errors, and begin using asynchronous programming paradigms. You'll learn how to create your own data types, and create object-oriented applications using classes and structs.

All object-oriented programming languages provide the ability to build your own custom classes. Classes increase the level of modularity in your application, and promote code reuse. This lesson will cover the key skills you'll need to build robust, object-oriented applications with Swift.

Lesson Objectives

By the end of this lesson, you will be able to do the following:

- Define and call Swift functions
- Explain how to pass functions as parameters and argument labels
- Implement exception handling with do...catch and guard
- Use object-oriented features such as struct and class

Functions

In the program structure section in *Lesson 1*, we mentioned that functions are a key part of Swift's structure, and are units of code that can accept parameters and can return values. In this section, we'll dive into Swift functions, learning how to implement and call them in the course of a Swift application.

Before diving into Swift function syntax, we should summarize some key points about how functions are used in Swift, and in modern software development generally:

- Functions are units of code that carry out some specific task.

- In terms of lines of code, functions should be short. How many lines of code is a maximum for a function has been a topic of debate for decades. However, long functions often do not satisfy the specific task definition.

- All things being equal, it's better to have a complex process broken into smaller functions, rather than combined into a large, complex function.

- All things being equal, a function that references its parameters—but not global variables—is more maintainable, less error-prone and more testable.

Defining a Function

For many developers new to Swift, its function declaration syntax may seem unfamiliar. Swift's function syntax is probably most similar to Pascal, but also has ideas from C++, Objective-C, and other programming languages. With some practice, Swift code will begin to feel elegant and familiar.

The basic syntax for a Swift function that accepts parameters is as follows:

```
func functionName(parm1: Type1, parm2: Type2) -> ReturnType {
```

The basic syntax for a Swift function that accepts no parameters is as follows:

```
func functionName() -> ReturnType {
```

The basic syntax for a Swift function that accepts no parameters and returns nothing is as follows:

```
func functionName() {
```

Let's break down the syntax:

- The keyword func signals that what follows is a function declaration. In Swift, there's no distinction between functions (that return a value) and procedures (which do not) — both begin with func.
- Following func is the *name* of the function. The naming rules for functions are the same as for Swift variables, and like variables, it's conventional to begin a function name with a lowercase letter.
- If the function accepts input parameters, they are listed within parentheses. Each parameter is followed by a colon (:) and then the data type of the parameter.
- If the function returns a value, the data type of the returned value is provided after an arrow formed by the hyphen and greater than characters (->).
- The beginning of the code block referenced by the function name begins at the opening brace character ({).

The following is a basic Swift function:

```
func printArray(array: [String]) -> Int {
    var count = 0
    for string in array {
        print(string)
        count += 1
    }
    return count
}
```

This function is defined with the name printArray. It accepts a single parameter — an array of String, which it will iterate and print. Finally, it returns a single Int value, which is the count of String values that it printed to the console.

Argument Labels

In the previous section, we created a function with a parameter named array, which is the parameter label we used when calling the function:

```
printArray(array: strings)
```

Swift supports optional argument labels for parameters, which will be familiar to Objective-C programmers, and likely unfamiliar to others.

Consider the following function, which returns the concatenation of two strings:

```
func concatenatedNames(n1: String, n2: String) -> String {
    return "\(n1) \(n2)"
}
```

While using short variable names within the function is convenient, calling the function may seem unintuitive from the point of view of the programmer calling the function:

```
let fullName = concatenatedNames(n1: "John", n2: "Smith")
```

Argument labels allow us to create a function that allows the caller of our function to refer to the function's parameters by different names than we use within the function.

For example, we might add argument labels to the function as follows:

```
func concatenatedNames(firstName n1: String, lastName n2: String) -> String
{
    return "\(n1) \(n2)"
}
```

Adding the argument labels doesn't change the implementation of the function at all—we still use the variable names n1 and n2 within the function. But the caller of the function may now use the more intuitive argument labels to refer to the parameter names:

```
let fullName = concatenatedNames(firstName: "John", lastName: "Smith")
```

Excluding Argument Labels

In addition to changing the calling reference for a function's parameters, argument labels can be used to remove names for input parameters. Doing so can make functions *feel* more like calling C or Objective-C functions.

For example, consider the following function:

```
func addTwoInts(_ a: Int, _ b: Int) -> Int {
    return x + y
}
```

By specifying the underscore (_) character for the argument label associated with each parameter, the caller need not specify a parameter name. The compiler will simply match each passed parameter to the function's passed parameter in the same order in which they are declared:

```
let c = addTwoInts(4, 5)    // c will be 9
```

> While excluding parameter names is a powerful feature, it should be used appropriately. Use this technique when the parameters passed to a function are obvious. For example: `addTwoInts(a,b)`, or `logMessage("Opened file")`. Don't use optional parameter names to make Swift *feel* more like you're using a programming language you've used in the past. The default Swift behavior — explicitly specifying parameter names — is intentional, and makes code easier to read, understand and maintain.

Parameter Default Values

Like many other C-inspired languages, you can provide parameter default values for any parameter. When a default value is specified in the function definition, the function caller can omit the parameter — and the default value will be substituted instead.

The following function prints the temperature. It assumes the provided value is in Centigrade units, if units are not specified:

```
enum TemperatureUnits : String {
    case celcius = "\u{00B0}C"
    case fahrenheit = "\u{00B0}F"
}

func printTemperature(value: Double, units: TempUnits = .celcius) {
    print("The temperature is \(value)\(units.rawValue)")
}
```

Because a default value is provided for units, we can omit the units when calling the function:

```
printTemperature(value: 17.5) // The temperature is 17.5°C
```

Activity: Implementing a Function

In any programming language, functions are a core language element used to make programs modular, readable, and maintainable, and virtually every program you write will use functions extensively. Let's practice what you've learned about Swift functions.

1. Launch Xcode and create a new playground, then save it to your desktop with the name Implement a Function.playground.

2. Add the following function to the playground:

```
func buildAddress(_ name: String, address: String, city: String, zipCode
postalCode: String, country: String? = "USA") -> String {

    return """
        \(name)
        \(address)
        \(city)
        \(postalCode)              \(country ?? "")
    """
}
```

3. Call the function within the print function twice, passing parameters as in the following code:

```
print(buildAddress("John Doe", address: "5 Covington Square", city:
"Birmingham", zipCode: "01234"))
print("=====")
print(buildAddress("John Doe", address: "5 Covington Square", city:
"Birmingham", zipCode: "01234", country: nil))
```

An example output is given here:

```
    John Doe
    5 Covington Square
    Birmingham
    01234
    USA
=====
    John Doe
    5 Covington Square
    Birmingham
    01234
```

Returning Values from Functions

Returning values from functions is largely consistent with C-inspired programming languages you've probably used in the past. When processing is finished, a function simply uses the `return` keyword to return a value to the caller. In the previous function example, we concatenated two String variables, and returned the result using the `return` keyword.

The following are some Swift-specific notes regarding returning values from functions:

- The value returned from the function must exactly match the return data type specified in the function definition. To avoid compile-time errors, convert or cast values that do not exactly match the return data type.

- It is allowed in Swift to use the `return` keyword anywhere in the function. You can return from more than one place in the function, when appropriate (such as in a `guard` statement, which we'll cover shortly).

- To return from a function that does not specify a return value, simply use the `return` keyword by itself.

- When a function returns no value, the `return` statement before the function's closing brace is optional.

- If a return value type is listed in the function definition, you must return a value of that type from every code path within the function. Failure to do so will generate a compiler error.

- While Swift functions can return only one value, that value can be a tuple, which can embed multiple other values together. For example, to return the three integers 2, 4, and 6 from a function, we can do the following:

```
return (2, 4, 6)
```

Swift can also return complex and custom types from functions. For example, your functions can return instances of structures, instances of classes, and references to other functions. So, while returning a single value may seem limiting, Swift actually provides tremendous flexibility in its function return features.

Using @discardableResult

The Swift compiler will generate a warning if you call a function that returns a result but do not use or assign that result in your code. For example, consider the following function:

```
func addTwoInts(_ a: Int, _ b: Int) -> Int {
   return x + y
}
```

Suppose we had called it with this line of code:

```
addTwoInts(4, 5)    // return is "discarded"
```

The Swift compiler doesn't understand why we would call a function that returns a value but not use that value. While not an error, it will generate a compile-time warning.

There are times when you may implement a function that returns a value which may not be important to the calling program. This is especially true when developing frameworks for use by other applications — where you provide functionality that the consumer of the framework may not feel is important to them.

For example, a `log()` function may return a Bool indicating how many characters of data were written to the log — even if the callers don't consider this information interesting:

```
func log(_ message: String) -> Int
```

Suppose the caller calls this function without using the Int return value:

```
log("app started!")
```

The compiler will generate the following warning:

```
Result of 'log(message:) is unused
```

To suppress the warning, simply add the `@discardableResult` function attribute with the declaration:

```
@disdcardableResult func log(_ message: String) -> Int
```

Now, knowing that you expect callers might disregard the return value, the Swift compiler will no longer issue a warning at the point of the function call.

Another way to suppress this warning is to assign the function return value to a placeholder, for example:

```
_ = log("app started")
```

In this syntax, the underscore character (_) is effectively a local variable with no name.

Function Attributes

In the previous section, we used the function attribute `discardableResult` to provide additional information to the Swift compiler about the usage of a function we declared. In that case, the `discardableResult` attribute informs the compiler that we expect callers of a function may ignore the value returned from the function.

You may encounter and use other function attributes in the course of your Swift programming. The following are some of the more common function attributes:

Name	Description
objc	Used to generate Objective-C calling wrappers. Used when a Swift function you write should also be callable from an Objective-C module.
nonobjc	Suppresses the generation of Objective-C compatibility wrappers where it otherwise would be created. Typically used to resolve circular references that occasionally occur between Swift and Objective-C modules.
available	Informs the compiler which OS versions, Swift versions, or platforms are required for a function to be called.
discardableResult	The return value may be ignored by function callers without generating a compiler warning message.
IBAction	Marks a function as a call point that can be connected to an Interface Builder design file.
introduced	The first version of the platform or language where this function was available.
deprecated	Marks a function as deprecated.

For more complete information about language attributes, refer to the Swift documentation at https://developer.apple.com/library/content/documentation/Swift/Conceptual/Swift_Programming_Language/Attributes.html.

Variadic Parameters

Swift supports functions with variadic parameters—these are named parameters that accept *more than one value of the same type.*

For example, we could write a function to make a sentence containing a variable number of words:

```
import Foundation
func makeSentence1(_ words: String...) -> String {
    var sentence = ""
    for word in words {
        sentence += "\(word) "
    }

    return "\(sentence.trimmingCharacters(in: [" "]))."
}
let sentence1 = makeSentence1("Hello", "World", "And", "Universe")
```

In this example, the makeSentence1 function will accept any number of words as input, and then uses the for...in loop to combine them into a sentence.

Because Swift's array features are quite powerful, and declaring an ad hoc array of values of the same type is quite easy, you might also approach variadic parameters in the following way:

```
func makeSentence2(_ words: [String]) -> String {
    var sentence = ""
    for word in words {
        sentence += "\(word) "
    }

    return "\(sentence.trimmingCharacters(in: [" "]))."
```

```
}
let sentence2 = makeSentence2(["Hello", "World", "And", "Universe"])
```

The output of both makeSentence1 and makeSentence2 is the same:

```
Hello World And Universe.
```

inout Parameters

In each example so far, when we've written a function that provided values back to the point of function call, we've used function return to do so. Using the return statement to return a new value to a function caller is the most common approach, and the approach you should use by default.

However, using return to send data back to the function's caller returns a new value. In some cases, it may be desirable to modify variables that are *owned* by the caller — rather than return new values. Swift provides inout parameters as a way to accomplish this.

Consider the following function, which swaps two Int values without inout parameters:

```
func swapValues1(_ a: Int, _ b: Int) -> (Int, Int) {
    return (b, a)
}
var a = 3
var b = 2

let (a1,b1) = swapValues1(a, b)

a = a1
b = b1

print("\(a), \(b)") // 2, 3
```

The parameters a and b are read-only within the function, and swapValues cannot change them. Instead, the function allocates a new tuple and returns it with the values in a swapped order. The caller assigns these new values into the tuple (a1, b1). The caller must then reassign the values of a and b to achieve the desired result.

By using `inout` parameters, we can write a function that can modify the values of the parameter values, and allow it to make the changes on behalf of the code in the calling scope:

```
var a = 3
var b = 2
func swapValues2(_ a: inout Int, _ b: inout Int) {
    let temp = a
    a = b
    b = temp
}
swapValues2(&a, &b)
print("\(a), \(b)") // 2, 3
```

In the `swapValues2` version, the `inout` keyword makes the parameters a and b read/write variables, so the code can reassign their values.

When calling `inout` parameters, an ampersand (&) must be placed before the variable being passed into the function. If you've used C or C++, you may recognize this syntax, which in those languages means *the address of*. The effect is the same as in those languages — the callee of the function is given permission to change the content of the variable provided as a parameter.

Recursion

Like many modern programming languages, Swift supports recursive function calls. Recursion is simply the ability for a function to call itself from within its own body. Most canonical use cases for recursion come from computer science, for example, sorting algorithms. However, even if you're an end user app developer, there may be times when recursion will make your code more concise and efficient.

The following function uses recursion to calculate the mathematical factorial:

```
func factorialWithRecursion(n: Int) -> Int {
    return n == 0 ? 1 : n * factorialWithRecursion(n: n-1)
}
```

The following line calls the recursive function, assigning the result to a variable named `factorial2`:

```
let factorial2 = factorialWithRecursion(n: 6) // 720
```

Functions as Parameters

Many languages, including Swift, have the ability to pass in functions by reference, which can then be called from within the called function. In many languages, the function passed as a parameter is referred to as a callback function, since it has the effect of allowing a function to call back to the caller's code to perform some action after the function has done what was asked of it.

In the following example, let's rewrite the `makeSentence` function with a version that passes in a callback function as a parameter:

```
import Foundation
func makeSentence3(_ words: [String], thenPrint: (String) -> Void) {
    var sentence = ""
    for word in words {
        sentence += "\(word) "
    }
    thenPrint("\(sentence.trimmingCharacters(in: [" "])).")
}

func printSentence(_ sentence: String) {
    print(sentence)
}

makeSentence3(["Hello", "World", "and", "Universe"], thenPrint:
printSentence(_:))
```

The output of this code is identical to `makeSentence1` and `makeSentence2` that we saw earlier.

In the *function as parameter* version 3, the `makeSentence3` function has no knowledge of how the printing will be done. It simply calls the function it's provided through the `thenPrint` parameter, and calls it when the sentence is finished.

The function as parameter technique is commonly used in scenarios where there may be more than one predefined alternative ending for a program flow. In the preceding example, we could have one `printSentence` routine that printed to the console, a second that posted the result to a web service, and a third that displayed a message box.

Functions as parameters are very powerful and flexible, and are commonly used in Swift programming. Next, we'll learn about a similar—and even more commonly used variant of this technique: **closures**.

Closures

In the previous section, you learned how to pass a named function into another function, allowing the latter to call the former at the appropriate time.

Closures are another way to pass code to a function, which it can then call later. In the case of closures, however, we're passing a block of code that can be called from within the function.

The two approaches are very similar—and to some extent, interchangeable. In both cases, the called function will run a block of code using the name specified by its own parameter name. A closure is primarily different in that a function as parameter *has a name* in the caller's scope, while a closure is an *unnamed* block of code.

Closures in Swift are the most common approach to providing code to execute after asynchronous processing has completed. The following function uses a closure to download data from the web. You'll fully implement this solution in the following activity:

```swift
func doWebRequest(closure: @escaping (_ webSiteContent: String?) -> Void) {
        let url = URL(string: "https://www.packtpub.com")!
        let urlRequest = URLRequest(url: url)
        let session = URLSession(configuration: URLSessionConfiguration.
default)

        let task = session.dataTask(with: urlRequest) {
            (data, response, error) in
            let content = String(data: data!, encoding: .utf8)
            closure(content)
        }
        task.resume()
    }
```

This ends our look at functions. In this section, we took a deep dive into how Swift implements functions and the importance of functions in developing virtually any application in Swift.

Creating a Function to Receive Content from an Asynchronous Web Service Call

For application developers who use any type of web service, processing the results of asynchronous web service requests will be a daily requirement. Let's apply what you've learned about writing functions to implement real-world web service requests:

1. Launch Xcode, and open the start project named `Functions - Starter.xcodeproj`.

2. Add the following function to the `ViewController.swift` file before the closing brace of the `ViewController` class:

```
func doWebRequest() -> String {
    var webPageContent = "No data yet!"

    let url = URL(string: "https://www.packtpub.com")!
    let urlRequest = URLRequest(url: url)
    let session = URLSession(
        configuration: URLSessionConfiguration.default)

    let task = session.dataTask(with: urlRequest) {
        (data, response, error) in
        webPageContent = String(data: data!, encoding: .utf8)!
    }
    task.resume()

    return webPageContent
}
```

3. Change the start project's `startButtonTapped` method to contain the following body:

```
@IBAction func startButtonTapped(_ sender: UIButton) {
    self.updateTextView(doWebRequest())
}
```

4. Run the application with a simulator, press the **Start Web Request** button, and observe the output in the `TextView` underneath the button.

    ◦ What happened? Why didn't that work?

    ◦ The `doWebRequest` function, as written, doesn't wait for the web request to complete before returning the `webPageContent` String variable.

5. Replace the doWebRequest function with the following implementation:

```swift
func doWebRequest(closure: @escaping (_ webSiteContent: String?)
-> Void) {
    let url = URL(string: "https://www.packtpub.com")!
    let urlRequest = URLRequest(url: url)
    let session = URLSession(configuration: URLSessionConfiguration.
default)

    let task = session.dataTask(with: urlRequest) {
        (data, response, error) in
        let content = String(data: data!, encoding: .utf8)
        closure(content)
    }
    task.resume()
}
```

  ○   This function accepts a closure parameter (named closure). In this
      implementation, the function doWebRequest has no return value. Instead,
      it waits until the web request has completed, and then returns the HTML
      response by calling the closure function, passing the HTML to the closure
      as a parameter value.

6. Modify the startButtonTapped function as follows, so that it calls the new
   doWebRequest version, which accepts a closure parameter:

```swift
@IBAction func startButtonTapped(_ sender: UIButton) {
    doWebRequest { (content) in
            self.updateTextView(content!)
    }
}
```

7. Run the application on a simulator, press the **Start Web Request** button, and
   observe the output in the debug console. You should now see the HTML source for
   the web page assigned to the url variable.

Assuming you encountered no exceptions or web connectivity problems, the program
you coded for the web request activity will have worked just fine. But it lacks any error
handling and is not up to scratch to include in a production application!

Open the project in the Functions – Finished with Error Handling folder, and
review it. Then, ask yourself what steps have been taken to ensure this code will not crash
the application when external data is not returned as expected.

Error Handling

We ended the last section by examining some sample code after it had been made production-quality by adding correct error handling techniques. In this section, we'll dig into the most common Swift error handling techniques, which will help ensure all the code you develop in Swift will be robust and of high quality.

Swift supports many of the same error handling techniques available in other object-oriented languages, such as C++, Java, and C#. Functions—either your own or standard library functions—often return error codes as integers, error types, and Boolean variables. In addition, Swift provides exception handling using the do...catch construction, which is functionally equivalent to the try...catch construction used in many other languages.

The do...catch Statement

Most modern languages have exception handling features that allow code to throw exceptions from an inner scope that can be caught in an outer scope. In Swift, this pattern is implemented using the do...catch structure.

You'll very often use the Swift do...catch structure when calling underlying Apple frameworks to do data processing or file access work on your behalf. Catching exceptions can help *bubble up* highly detailed error information to your code.

The following code declares a block that calls a function decode, which may throw an exception of type Error:

```
do {
    let userObject = try decode()
    print(userObject.name)
} catch let error {
    print(error)
}
```

The important thing to note is that the code in between do and catch doesn't explicitly check for an error. It simply instructs the decode function to try to complete successfully. In the event that decode encounters an error, the remainder of the do block will be skipped and the catch block will receive the thrown Error object, assigning it to the local variable error.

Multiple catch Blocks

In practice, a function that throws an exception may throw one of several more specific exceptions, depending on what went wrong.

The do...catch construction allows you to catch more than one exception type. This works almost identically to constructing a switch statement with multiple case code blocks.

Multiple catch blocks provide the program with more specific information about the cause of the decoding error, if available, for example:

```
func decodeWithException() {
    if let data = jsonText.data(using: String.Encoding.utf8) {
        let decoder = JSONDecoder()

        do {
            let userObject = try decoder.decode(UserInfo.self,
                                                from: data)
            print("User decoded form JSON: \(userObject)")
        } catch let DecodingError.typeMismatch(_, context) {
            print("Type Mismatch Error: \(context.debugDescription)")
        } catch let DecodingError.dataCorrupted(context) {
            print("Decoding Error: \(context.debugDescription)")
        } catch let error {
            print(error.localizedDescription)
        }

        print("program always continues from this point.")
    }
}
```

Using do without catch

What if you didn't want to catch an exception, but wanted your program to continue even when an exception is thrown?

By using the try? keyword (that is, try with a question mark after it), we can ask Swift to try to run code that may throw an exception, and return the result as an optional variable. In this case, if an exception is thrown, the returned optional will be nil; if no exception is thrown, the optional will contain the value the function would normally return, for example:

```
do {
    let userObject = try? decode()
    print(userObject?.name)
}
```

In this case, if the decode function throws an exception, the userObject optional will be nil, and the print(userObject.name) line will not be executed. Because the action taken if an exception is thrown is to assign nil to the variable on the left-hand side of the equal sign, it's no longer necessary to wrap the decode call in the do...catch block.

The guard Statement

The guard statement is most commonly used at the top of a function body to validate that the data the function will use to complete its task is in an expected state. In this sense, the guard statement acts as a guard at the gate—checking the contents of inputs to the function before they're allowed in.

In early versions of Swift, we didn't have the `guard` statement, and it was common to implement functions structured like the following:

```
func printAddress1(zipCode: String?,
           countryCode: String?, areaCode: String?) -> Bool {
    if let zip = zipCode, let country = countryCode,
                                    let area = areaCode {
        if zip.count != 5 {
            return
        }
        if country.count != 2 {
            return
        }
        if area.count != 3 {
            return
        }
        print("\(zip), \(country), \(area)")
    }
}
```

While this function isn't too difficult to follow, it can become confusing for the reader where the ending brace of the `if let { }` block ends.

Developers would frequently reduce the editor font to a tiny size to try to make out where in the sequence of ending braces the close of the original error checking `if let` block ended!

The `guard` keyword is effectively a clearer version of this structure—moving the closing braces of validations together in neat code blocks. An equivalent function using the `guard` syntax is as follows:

```
func printAddress(zipCode: String?,
           countryCode: String?, areaCode: String?) {
    guard let zip = zipCode, zip.count == 5 else { return }

    guard let country = countryCode,
                        country.count == 2 else { return }

    guard let area = areaCode, area.count == 3 else { return }

    print("\(zip), \(country), \(area)")
}
```

In the second version, the guard statement makes the code more readable, and moves all the state-checking code to the beginning of the function where it can be easily reviewed and understood.

We have reached the end of this section. Here, we focused on error handling and exception handling, as implemented in Swift. To reiterate, Swift uses do...catch instead of try...catch and also allows us to use multiple catch blocks.

Activity: Exception Handling

Exception handling, as the name implies, is an error handling technique that enables you to let the Swift compiler know what errors you expect, and provide a way to *listen* for them if they occur while your program is running. We'll now apply exception handling in one of the most common use cases for application developers — parsing data structures from JSON into application data structures.

In this activity, we'll use an Xcode playground to practice catching an exception while parsing a JSON string into a custom data structure — a very common task in any application development work that involves integration with web services.

1. Launch Xcode and create a new playground, then save it to your desktop with the name ExceptionHandling.playground.

2. Add the following import to the top of the playground file:

    ```
    import Foundation
    ```

3. Add the following code to define a data structure that holds basic user information for an application:

    ```
    struct UserInfo : Codable {
        var name: String
        var email: String
        var userId: String
    }
    ```

4. Now add the following `decodeJson` function to decode a JSON string:

```swift
func decodeJson(jsonText: String) {
    if let data = jsonText.data(using: String.Encoding.utf8) {
        let decoder = JSONDecoder()

        do {
            let userObject =
                try decoder.decode(UserInfo.self, from: data)

            print("User decoded form JSON: \(userObject)")
        } catch let error {
            print(error.localizedDescription)
        }
    }
    print("program always continues from this point.")
}
```

5. Add the following statement to call the `decodeJson` function with a data string that almost correctly matches the expected data structure keys (the name field has the wrong case):

```swift
decodeJson(jsonText : "{ \"Name\" : \"John Smith\", \"email\" : \"john@
smith.com\", \"userId\" : \"jsmith\"}")
```

6. Observe the exception printed to the debug console.

7. Modify the string to correct the uppercase letter in the name field, and observe that the properly encoded JSON object is printed in the console.

Because the `jsonText` data is not in the correct format (the name field cannot begin with an uppercase letter), the `decoder.decode` function throws an exception. The exception is caught in the `catch` block, reporting an error. You eliminate the exception by changing the case of the name field in the `jsonText` string.

Object-Oriented Features

Throughout the past couple of lessons, we've been learning how to use Swift syntax, variables, functions, and control flow structures to develop the building blocks of Swift applications. In the final section of this lesson, we'll learn how to pull all those language components together into Swift's object-oriented classes and structures—the high-level building blocks of most professional Swift applications.

Object-Oriented Principles

Swift is an object-oriented programming language, and enables the core principles of object-oriented programming. Generally speaking, in object-oriented programming, variables, functions and data structures that implement a functional unit of your program are combined into an *object* that exists within its own namespace, and is accessed by other objects through filtered, publicly exposed interfaces.

Using Swift, instances are created using both **structs** and **classes**. Structs and classes support encapsulation and abstraction, though only classes support inheritance. Both object types — structs and classes — are frequently used in Swift, and neither is *better* than the other for all use cases.

Classes Versus Structs

Virtually all object-oriented languages are based on the concept of organizing units of code into classes that perform a very specific set of actions on a specific set of data.

Illustration

A *class* can be thought of as a pattern, such as one a clothes factory might place over a bolt of fabric to cut a new shirt. The pattern (class) has all the dimensions and notations that describe to the tailor what shape the shirt will take. The tailor can use the pattern to create as many shirts as they need — each one perfectly formed by placing the pattern on the raw fabric and cutting around the pattern. Here, the tailor is the Swift runtime, the pattern is the class (or struct) designed by the programmer, and the finished shirt is an object generated by the Swift runtime environment.

While this section isn't a comprehensive tutorial on object-oriented programming, some general guidelines for selecting between classes and structs are the following:

- Structs are *value types*, which are always copied when passed between objects or assigned to variables. This makes them ideal to use when creating objects that are primarily used to store data structures (though structs can and do include functions that operate on their data).
- Classes support inheritance, which makes them the only alternative when defining objects that will serve as base classes or be derived from base classes.
- Classes, as reference types, are also a better choice when it's advantageous to pass an object by reference, allowing its members to be directly modified by functions it's passed to (this is somewhat similar to the `inout` parameter distinction we learned earlier in this lesson).

Defining Classes and Structures

In this lesson, we'll focus on the syntax to define, instantiate, and use your own structs and classes. These techniques are nearly the same for each object type.

A class or struct is defined with the following syntax:

- The `struct` or `class` keyword defines a namespace for the class. This namespace is prepended to any symbol definition within the scope of the struct or class when your application is assembled.

- The definition of struct or class members is enclosed in braces ({...}).

- If a class or struct contains member variables that are not assigned default values where defined, an initializer must be provided so the uninitialized member variables can be assigned a value. For structs (but not for classes), the Swift compiler will create an initializer for you.

- Within the definition braces, variables and functions can be added, according to the techniques learned in the last couple of lessons.

- Classes, structs, and their enclosed methods and variables can be given specific access levels, which control how visible they will be from outside modules. The default access level is `Internal`, which makes all elements visible to any code in the same module.

The following are declarations for a `Customer` object—the first declared as a struct and the second as a class:

```
struct Customer {
    var name: String
    var customerNumber: String
}

class Customer {
    var name: String
    var customerNumber: String
}
```

Throughout the last couple of lessons, you've been using structs and classes, for example:

- The String type is a struct that contains many properties and functions—for example, the `.count` property we often used to count the characters contained in a string.

- We used the `JSONDecoder` class to decode the JSON text in *Activity B*.

As you develop applications with Swift, you'll use classes and structs frequently, and will often define your own.

Next, you'll solidify your understanding of basic struct and class usage by practicing the creation of each type of object in an activity.

Activity: Creating a Customer Struct and Class

To compare the differences (and similarities) between Swift classes and structs, it's useful to implement the same data structure in both. This is exactly what we'll do now.

Use an Xcode playground to practice how to create Swift structs and classes.

1. Launch Xcode and create a new playground, then save it to your desktop with the name `CustomerStructClass.playground`.

2. Add the following lines of code to declare a new `Customer` struct:

   ```
   struct CustomerStruct {
   }
   ```

3. Below the closing brace of the struct definition, create a new variable of type `Customer`. Congratulations! You've created a struct definition, and instantiated your first custom object!

   ```
   var customer1 = CustomerStruct()
   ```

4. Modify the code to the following, adding the enum `CustomerType` and variable `type` to the struct. Then modify your code to print the current `customer.type` to the debug console:

   ```
   struct CustomerStruct {
       enum CustomerType: String {
           case gold = "Gold Customer!"
           case silver = "Silver Customer!"
           case unknown = "Unknown customer type"
       }

       var type: CustomerType?
   }

   var customer1 = CustomerStruct()

   print(customer1.type ?? "invalid customer type")
   ```

      ◦   At this point, the `print` statement prints **invalid customer type**, because the member variable within the struct is initialized to an optional having a `nil` value.

5. Because this is a struct, Swift has auto-created an initializer we can use to set an initial value for the customer value. Modify the instantiation of the `customer` variable as follows:

```
var customer = CustomerStruct(type: .gold)
```

      ◦   Now when the code runs, the output is the string **gold**.

6. Creating a similar data structure as a class is quite similar. Add the following class definition to your playground:

```
class CustomerClass {
    enum CustomerType: String {
        case gold = "Gold Customer!"
        case silver = "Silver Customer!"
        case unknown = "Unknown customer type"
    }

    var type: CustomerType?

    init(type:CustomerType) {
        self.type = type
    }
}
```

      ◦   This definition declares a class of type `CustomerClass`. Because Swift does not automatically create initializers for classes, `CustomerClass` includes an initializer to allow its `CustomerType` variable to be set on instantiation—just as the automatically created struct initializer does for `CustomerStruct`.

7. Finally, add the following two lines to the playground to instantiate an object of type `CustomerClass`, and print its `type` enum member to the debug console:

```
var customer2 = CustomerClass(type: .silver)
print(customer2.type ?? "invalid customer type")
```

Summary

In the last couple of lessons, you've learned all the key building blocks needed to build feature-rich, robust Swift programs:

- In *Lesson 1, Swift Basics*, you learned key language basics: using variables, optionals, data types, and essential Swift code syntax
- In *Lesson 2, Swift Operators and Control Flow*, you learned the fundamental structures you need to build logic and express the core flow of your application: control flow, looping structures, and the range of operators Swift supports
- In this lesson, you began taking your Swift skills to the next level by creating functions, handling exceptions, and defining your own data types using struct and class language features

In the next couple of lessons, you'll continue to build your Swift knowledge by learning more advanced language concepts, including the following:

- Using and extending Swift collections
- Using Swift's sophisticated and powerful Unicode String structure and protocols
- Using Swift's functional programming and lazy operations features

Challenge

We'll tie together a variety of Swift language techniques, giving you additional practice to create structs, functions, data types, and optionals, and use flow control structures.

To solidify your understanding of basic struct and class usage by practicing the creation of each type of object.

1. Launch Xcode, and create a new playground, then save it to your desktop with the name `Activity 5 - Final Activity.playground`.
2. Add the following enum, which will be used to classify customers by gold, silver, and platinum levels. Note that this enum has a `rawValue` of type String, which we will use while printing customer information:

```
enum CustomerType:String {
    case silver = "SILVER"
    case gold = "GOLD"
    case platinum = "PLATINUM"
}
```

3. Create a new `Customer` struct with a set of String variables, including an optional for `country` and the variable `type` to classify the customer into one of the `CustomerType` categories:

```
struct Customer {
    var name: String
    var address: String
    var city: String
    var state: String
    var country: String?
    var type: CustomerType
}
```

4. Within the `Customer` struct, add an enum `OutputType` to control customer printing output style as either a formatted label, a debug output, or both. This enum has no `rawValue`:

```
enum OutputType {
    case label, debug, both
}
```

5. Add a function `printAddress` to the `Customer` struct that can be called to print customer address information in a variety of styles. This function returns a result, but includes the `@discardableResult` annotation so that callers who do not store its return value won't generate a compiler warning. This function also allows (but does not require) additional text lines to be appended to the end of the address label output via a variadic parameter:

```
@discardableResult func printAddress(outputType: OutputType = .label,
additionalLines: String?...) -> OutputType {

    switch outputType {
        case .both:
            printDebug()
            fallthrough
        case .label:
            printLabel(additionalLines)
        case .debug:
            printDebug()
    }

    return outputType
}
```

6. Add a function `printLabel` to the `Customer` struct that creates a formatted string and prints it to the console. Note that this function is declared as `private` so that it can be called only from other functions in the `Customer` class (forcing callers to go through the `printAddress` function to print label data). This function also accepts an array of optional strings:

```
private func printLabel(_ additionalLines: [String?]) {
    var addressString = """
        \(type.rawValue)
        \(name)
        \(address)
        \(city), \(state)
        """

    if let countryText = country {
        addressString += "\n\(countryText)"
    }
    for line in additionalLines {
        if let line = line {
            // "line" and "line" have the same name, but exist in
different scopes.
            // The inner 'line' variable is a non-Optional, scoped
within this block,
            //and is created only when the Optional 'line' variable
created by the for statement is not nil
            addressString += "\n\(line)"
        }
    }

    print(addressString)
}
```

7. Add a function `printDebug` to the `Customer` class to print a simple output string to the console. This function will be called when the `printAddress` function is called with either the `.debug` or `.both` style parameters:

```
private func printDebug() {
    print(self)
}
```

8. Add a function `customerTuple` to return customer information as a tuple containing six unnamed members:

```
func customerTuple() -> (String, String, String, String, String?,
String) {
    return (name, address, city, state, country, type.rawValue)
}
```

9. Now create two `Customer` objects, `customer1` and `customer2`, with different address information:

```
let customer1 = Customer(name: "John Doe", address: "100 First Street",
city: "Springfield", state: "Indiana", country: "USA", type: .platinum)

let customer2 = Customer(name: "Jane Doe", address: "57 Morgan Circle",
city: "Las Vegas", state: "Nevada", country: "USA", type: .silver)
```

10. Create a constant variable `tuple`, and assign it the return of the `customerTuple` function:

```
let tuple = customer1.customerTuple()
```

11. Print the first and third members of the tuple (customer name and address):

```
print("Customer named ", tuple.0, " lives in ", tuple.2)
```

12. Call the `printAddress` function on the `customer2` object, directing the function to print a formatted label with two additional lines under the address:

```
customer2.printAddress(outputType: .label, additionalLines: "C/O Sam
Johnson", "Forwarding Requested")
```

13. Call the `printAddress` function on the `customer2` object, this time passing the `.debug` style parameter, and no additional lines:

```
customer2.printAddress(outputType: .debug)
```

14. Finally, call the `printAddress` function on the `customer1` object, this time passing the `.both` style parameter. The `printAddress` function's `switch` statement will use the `fallthrough` instruction to print both versions of the address output:

```
customer1.printAddress(outputType: .both)
```

4

Collections

In the previous lesson, we looked into building Swift functions, error handling, and developing fully-featured Swift programs. We also briefly looked at a few OOP features.

In this lesson, we will work extensively with Swift's collections, such as arrays, sets, and dictionaries.

The Swift Standard Library (`https://developer.apple.com/documentation/swift`) is automatically imported into all Swift code, and contains basic types such as `Int`, `Double`, `Bool`, `Optional`, and more. It is primarily organized around protocols, because Swift is a Protocol-Oriented language (`https://developer.apple.com/videos/play/wwdc2015/408/`).

The root protocol for collections, which they all inherit from, is `Sequence`. All a type needs to conform to it is the ability to provide one value at a time, until it is empty, at which point it will output `nil`. This simple requirement provides a long list of methods (`https://developer.apple.com/documentation/swift/sequence#topics`), and lets you iterate over the type with a `for...in` loop:

```
for element in somesequence {
  // do something with 'element'
}
```

Collection (`https://developer.apple.com/documentation/swift/collection`) inherits from `Sequence`, and adds the ability to refer to a specific position in the collection with an index. You can go forwards from an index, until you reach the end. Unlike `Sequence`, it guarantees that you can iterate over it multiple times. In other words, it preserves its contents, whereas a `Sequence` may forget each value as soon as it has provided it:

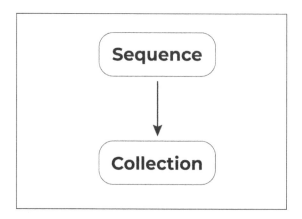

It is worth noting that, like practically everything else in the Standard Library, all of the collections are value types (`https://developer.apple.com/library/ content/documentation/Swift/Conceptual/Swift_Programming_Language/ ClassesAndStructures.html#//apple_ref/doc/uid/TP40014097-CH13-ID88`). That means they are not reference types (pointers), like classes, so no two identifiers ever refer to the same value.

Lesson Objectives

By the end of this lesson, you will be able to do the following:

- Use the main collections in the Swift Standard Library: arrays, sets, and dictionaries
- Explain sequences, collections, and other useful protocols
- Create extensions of the standard library, as well as new types

Arrays

An array is an ordered collection of elements of the same type, and they are used for pretty much anything that requires storing things in a certain order, such as the contents of lists in apps. It works like similar types in other languages.

Working with Arrays

Here are some of the most common operations on arrays:

- Create an array:
  ```
  let a = [0,1,2,3,4] // array literal
  ```

- Join two arrays:
  ```
  var b = a + [5,6]
  ```

- Repeat a value:
  ```
  let c = Array(repeating: 4.1, count: 3)
  ```

- Create an array from any sequence (a String is a Sequence of Character):
  ```
  var d = Array("The ☀ and ☽ ")
  ```

- Add values to the end of an array:
  ```
  b.append(10) // append one element
  ```

- Append an entire array:
  ```
  b += a
  b.append(contentsOf: a) // append a sequence
  ```

- Get the length of an array:
  ```
  b.count
  ```

- Iterate over all elements:

```
for nr in b {
        // do something with 'nr'
        }
```

Here are their abilities, represented by some of the protocols they conform to:

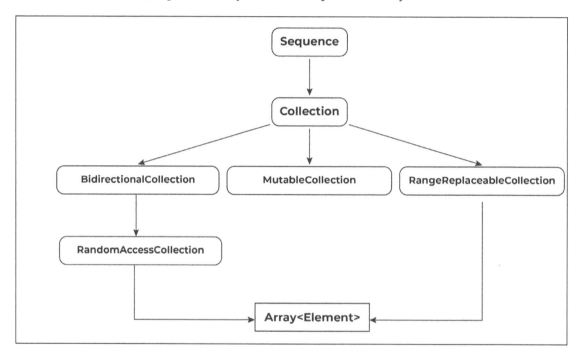

- `BidirectionalCollection` can go backwards from any index (except for the first one).
- `MutableCollection` can replace any element with a different one, but can't necessarily change the length of the collection.
- `RangeReplaceableCollection` can add and remove elements, and create a new empty instance of itself.

- RandomAccessCollection does not offer any new methods over BidirectionalCollection, but it guarantees that accessing any part of the collection takes the same amount of time, no matter how big it is. Array can do this because all of its elements are the same size, so it can instantly calculate where they are in memory.

Index

You use indices to refer to specific positions in an Array. The index type of an Array is Int (integer), and its startIndex is always 0. Its endIndex is the same as the length of the array. You can think of an index as something that's pointing to the space between elements, right before the element it refers to. Here is an array of characters:

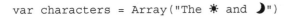

```
var characters = Array("The ☀ and ☾")
```

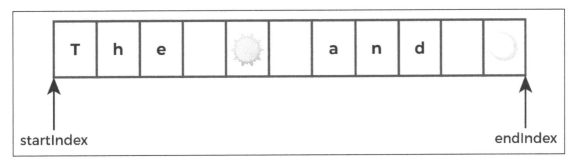

endIndex points to the position *after* the end, so if you ever try to access an element at endIndex with characters[characters.endIndex] (or with any other invalid index), your program will crash. If an array is empty, startIndex and endIndex are both 0.

Common Operations with Index

Here are some common operations using indices:

- Read an element at a particular index:

  ```
  characters[2] // read element at index 2 ("e")
  ```

- Change the element at a particular index:

  ```
  characters[2] = "a" // change element at index 2
  ```

- Remove and return an element at a particular index:

  ```
  let removed = characters.remove(at: 8)
  ```

- Insert an element at a particular index:

  ```
  characters.insert("i", at: 7)
  ```

- Insert a collection of elements at a particular index:

  ```
  characters.insert(contentsOf: "t the", at: 9)
  ```

- Print all elements:

  ```
  print(characters)
  // ["T", "h", "a", " ", "☀", " ", "a", "i", "n", "t", " ", "t",
  "h", "e", " ", "☽"]
  ```

Many collections use their own custom index type instead of Int, and even those that use Int do not necessarily have a startIndex that is always 0. It is therefore recommended to always use an array's startIndex instead of 0. This also makes the code clearer.

As with all indices, note that they may become invalid or point to the wrong element if the Array is mutated after they are created. To check if an index can still be used, all collections have an `indices` property, which is a collection of all the current indices:

```
characters.indices.contains(index)
```

ArraySlice

All sequences have a `SubSequence`, a type which represents a subrange of its elements. `Array.SubSequence` is `ArraySlice`:

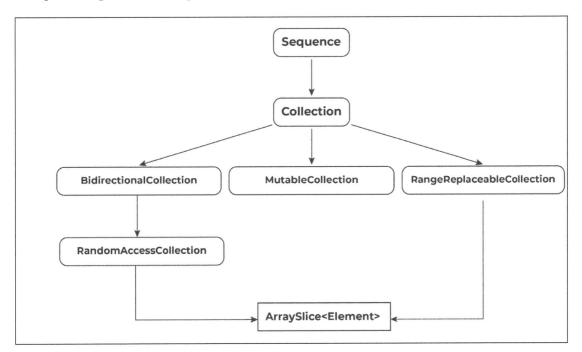

It has the same heritage and API as Array. It keeps a reference to the array it was created from, and its startIndex and endIndex represent the subrange within the array:

```
let characters = Array("The ☀ and ☽ ")
let slice = characters[4..<9]
print(slice) // ["☀", " ", "a", "n", "d"]
```

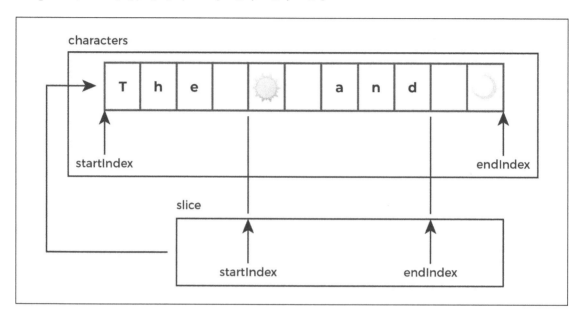

This allows us to have just one copy of a big array in memory, and use slices as views onto it. But each slice holds on to the array, so if you want to keep a slice around for a while, it is recommended to convert it to an array (using Array(slice)). This will copy the elements of the slice to its own array and release the reference, allowing the big array to be freed if nothing else holds on to it.

If you mutate the array or the slice after the slice has been created, a copy will be made automatically and the change will not be reflected in the other.

Creating Slices

Use the `prefix()` and `suffix()` functions to create slices with the leading and trailing elements of the array:

- Create a slice with the first three elements:

      characters.prefix(3)

- Create a slice with all elements before the first space:

      characters.prefix(while: {$0 != " "})

- Create a slice with the last two elements:

      characters.suffix(2) // the last two elements

- Create a slice with all elements from index 4:

      characters.suffix(from: 4)

We can also use ranges to create slices:

- Create a slice from indices 2 to 4 inclusive:

      characters[2...4]

- Create a slice from index 3 up to, but not including 6:

      characters[3..<6]

- Create a slice from index 3 to the end:

      characters[3...]

- Create a slice from the beginning up to and including index 5:

      characters[...5]

- Create a slice from the beginning up to but not including index 5:

      characters[..<5]

- Create a slice of the entire array:

      characters[...]

Activity: Working with Arrays

Many operations on arrays can be done far more efficiently if the array is sorted. We will add methods that take advantage of this for insertion, finding the index of the first or last occurrence of an element, and checking if the array contains an element.

We will just add methods to an array in an extension, but ideally this should be its own type with an internal array so that we can guarantee it is always sorted. Check out `https://github.com/ole/SortedArray` for an example of this.

1. Open the `CollectionsExtra` Xcode project, and go to `SortedArray.swift`.

2. Create an extension to Range to find the middle of it. This will be used with the indices of the array:

    ```
    public extension Range where Bound == Int {
      /// The value in the middle of this range. Returns nil if the range is
    empty.
      var middle: Int? {
        guard !isEmpty else { return nil }
        return lowerBound + count / 2
      }
    }
    ```

3. We will assume that the array has been sorted using the < operator (ascending), and we will assure that elements can be used with this operator by constraining the extension to arrays with elements that adopt the `Comparable` protocol. This also means they can be used with >, ==, !=, >=, and <=:

    ```
    extension Array where Element: Comparable {
    ```

4. Next, we need to find the insertion point if we were to insert an element into the sorted array. We can use this for insertion and checking if the array contains a specific element. This is a standard binary search, implemented with recursion:

    ```
    /// The index to use if you were to insert this element into a sorted
    array.
    ///
    /// - Parameters:
    ///   - element: The element to potentially insert.
    ///   - range: The range to search in.
    /// - Note: If the element already occurs once or more, the index to
    one of those will be returned.
    func insertionIndex(for element: Element, in range: Range<Index>) ->
    Index {
    ```

```
   guard let middle = range.middle else { return range.upperBound }
   if self[middle] < element {
     return insertionIndex(for: element, in: index(after:
middle)..<range.upperBound)
   } else if self[middle] > element {
     return insertionIndex(for: element, in: range.lowerBound..<middle)
   }
   return middle
 }
```

Note that when returning `middle`, we do not check if the element in that position is the one we are searching for. This is because the `Comparable` protocol demands that if an element is neither bigger than nor smaller than another element, then they must be equal.

The range will normally start as the entire array.

5. Inserting an element is now very simple:

```
/// Inserts the element in the correct position in a sorted array.
///
/// - Parameter element: The element to insert.
/// - Returns: The index where the element was inserted.
@discardableResult
public mutating func sorted_insert(_ element: Element) -> Index {
  let index = insertionIndex(for: element, in: startIndex..<endIndex)
  self.insert(element, at: index)
  return index
}
```

6. When checking if the array contains a specific element, we can first get the insertion index, check that it is not the `endIndex` (if the element does not exist and is larger than all the other elements), and see if the element at the index is the one we are searching for:

```
/// Checks if a sorted array contains an element.
public func sorted_contains(_ element: Element) -> Bool {
  let index = insertionIndex(for: element, in: startIndex..<endIndex)
  return (index != endIndex) && (self[index] == element)
}
```

7. When searching for the first occurrence of an element in the array, we can't use `insertionIndex`. This is because if the element occurs more than once, it may return the index to any of those occurrences. Instead, we will use a slightly modified version (`https://github.com/raywenderlich/swift-algorithm-club/blob/master/Count%20Occurrences/README.markdown`):

```
/// The index of the first occurrence of this element in a sorted
array.
///
/// - Parameters:
///    - element: The element to search for.
///    - range: The range to search within.
/// - Returns: The index, or nil if not found.
public func sorted_index(of element: Element, in range: Range<Index>?
= nil) -> Index? {
   let range = range ?? startIndex..<endIndex
   guard let middle = range.middle else {
     let index = range.upperBound
     return (self.indices.contains(index) && self[index] == element) ?
index : nil
   }
   if self[middle] < element {
     return sorted_index(of: element, in: index(after: middle)..<range.
upperBound)
   }
   return sorted_index(of: element, in: range.lowerBound..<middle)
}
```

The main difference is that we only check if the element in the middle is less than what we are searching for, not both less than and greater than, like in `insertionIndex`. We can do this because, in a sorted array, all equal elements are grouped together. Even if `middle` happens to point to an equal element, there may still be more of those to the *left*, so we continue searching there. If there aren't, we still end up with the index in the correct place.

Since we are using properties of `self` for the default value of the `range` parameter, we cannot provide them in the function header. Instead, we set the default value to `nil`, and then create a new local variable called `range` which is set to the default value `startIndex..<endIndex` if no other value was provided when the function was called.

8. The code for finding the last index of an element is almost identical:

```
/// The index of the last occurrence of this element in a sorted
array.
///
/// - Parameters:
///   - element: The element to search for.
///   - range: The range to search within.
/// - Returns: The index, or nil if not found.
public func sorted_lastIndex(of element: Element, in range:
Range<Index>? = nil) -> Index? {
    let range = range ?? startIndex..<endIndex
    guard let middle = range.middle else {
        let index = self.index(before: range.upperBound)
        return (self.indices.contains(index) && self[index] == element) ?
index : nil
    }
    if self[middle] > element {
        return sorted_lastIndex(of: element, in: range.
lowerBound..<middle)
    }
    return sorted_lastIndex(of: element, in: index(after:
middle)..<range.upperBound)
    }
}
```

Here, we check if `middle` points to an element that is greater than what we are searching for. If it isn't, we go to the *right*. When we have finally found an index, we use the element before it.

9. Go to `SortedArrayTests.swift`, uncomment the unit tests, and run them all.

Sets

A set is an unordered collection of unique elements. It can very efficiently add, remove, or check if it contains a specific element (on average *O(1)*, meaning it takes the same time regardless of the size of the set), in contrast to an unsorted array, where these operations take *O(n)* (the array may need to access and/or move most of its element).

Sets can be used for tracking which part of a custom view should be hidden, like which parts of an outline view are collapsed. When displaying the view, you would only show the children of those nodes which are not in the *collapsed* set. So, you are in a sense adding a Bool property to types you do not control. Sets can also be used for removing duplicates; you just add a sequence to an empty set and all duplicates will be gone.

Set implements these protocols:

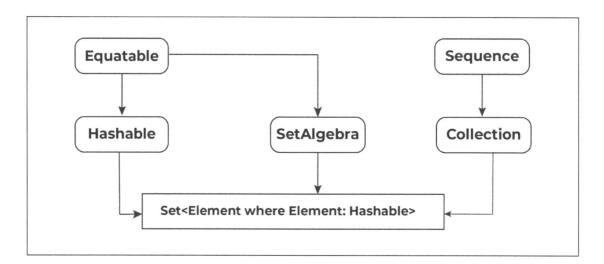

- Equatable means you can check if instances are equal with a == b or not equal with a != b. Each type defines for itself what *equal* means, and it doesn't necessarily mean *identical*.

- Hashable types have an integer property hashValue, which dictionaries and sets (among others) use to quickly find instances. Values that are equal always have the same hashValue.

- SetAlgebra has some mathematical set operations such as intersection, union, and subtraction.

 A Set is a Collection which has its own index type, but since Set is unordered, we hardly ever have a need for it.

All types used in a set have to conform to the `Hashable` protocol:

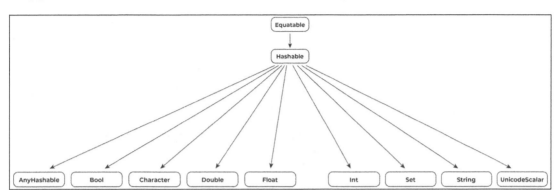

A lot of other types conform to `Hashable` (https://developer.apple.com/documentation/swift/hashable#adopted-by).

Working with Sets

To create a set and perform some common operations on it, follow these steps:

1. Create a set and print it to see that the order is not preserved:

   ```
   var numbers: Set = [0,1,2,3,10,2.75,-3,-3.125,-14]
   print(numbers) // [-3.125, 10.0, 2.75, 2.0, -3.0, 3.0, -14.0,
   0.0, 1.0]
   ```

2. Insert a value if nothing equal is already there:

   ```
   numbers.insert(4)
   ```

3. Insert, and replace it if something equal is already there:

   ```
   numbers.update(with: 4)
   ```

4. Some more common operations:

   ```
   numbers.remove(4)
   numbers.contains(3)
   numbers.isEmpty
   for n in numbers {
     // ...
   }
   ```

5. Run the code. This is what will appear on your screen:

```
var numbers: Set = [0,1,2,3,10,2.75,-3,-3.125,-14]          {10, -3.125, 2.75, 0, 2, 3, 1, -14, -3}

// order is not preserved
print(numbers)                                               "[10.0, -3.125, 2.75, 0.0, 2.0, 3.0, 1.0, -14.0, -3.0]\n"

// insert if nothing equal is already there
numbers.insert(4)                                            (inserted true, memberAfterInsert 4)

// insert, and replace it if something equal is already there
numbers.update(with: 4)                                      4

numbers.remove(4)                                            4
numbers.contains(3)                                          true
numbers.isEmpty                                              false

for n in numbers {
    n                                                        (9 times)
}
```

```
[10.0, -3.125, 2.75, 0.0, 2.0, 3.0, 1.0, -14.0, -3.0]
```

Combining Sets

Here's how to filter and combine different sets:

```
extension Double {
  var isInteger: Bool { return self.truncatingRemainder(dividingBy: 1) == 0 }
}
}

let negativenumbers = numbers.filter { $0 < 0 }
let positivenumbers = numbers.subtracting(negativenumbers.union([0]))

let integers = numbers.filter { $0.isInteger }
let negativeintegers = integers.intersection(negativenumbers)
print(negativeintegers) // [-3.0, -14.0]
```

union combines two sets. intersection returns the elements both sets have in common. symmetricDifference returns elements that are in either of the two sets, but not in both. subtracting returns elements of the first set that do not occur in the second set.

All of these have mutating versions that change the first set in-place (they all start with `form`, except for `subtract`. For more information, check out: `https://swift.org/documentation/api-design-guidelines/#name-according-to-side-effects`.)

Comparing Sets

Have a look at the following code:

```
// all of the following return "true"
numbers.isSuperset(of: negativeintegers)
integers.isSubset(of: numbers)
positivenumbers.isStrictSubset(of: numbers)
numbers.isStrictSuperset(of: negativenumbers)
negativenumbers.isDisjoint(with: positivenumbers)
```

Set A is a *superset* of set B if every member of B is also a member of A. This also makes B a *subset* of A. These are *strict* supersets/subsets if A contains at least one element that is not a member of B. In other words: a strict superset or subset means that the two sets are not equal. *Disjoint* means the two sets have no elements in common.

Activity: Removing Duplicates from a Sequence

The most common method of removing duplicates from a sequence is to just add the entire sequence to a set, and then create a new sequence from the set. However, this might re-order the remaining elements. Here, we will use `filter` to keep the original order, and use a set to keep track of which values are already in the sequence.

By adding the method as an extension to `Sequence`, it can be used by any collection type, including Array, Dictionary, and Set (though it would be rather pointless to use it on dictionaries and sets, as they are already duplicate-free).

1. Open the `CollectionsExtra` Xcode project we used earlier, and go to `Set.swift`.

2. Paste the following code in the Swift file:

```
extension Sequence where Element: Hashable {
    /// Returns an array containing each element in `self` only once, in
the same order.
    public func removeDuplicates () -> [Element] {
        var originals = Set<Element>(minimumCapacity: underestimatedCount)
        return self.filter { x in
            if originals.contains(x) {
                return false
            }
            originals.insert(x)
            return true
        }
    }
}
```

`filter` is a method of `Sequence`, which takes a function, `Element -> Bool`, and returns an array with only those elements for which the function returns `true`. In this function, we check if the element is already in the `originals` set. If it is, we return `false` (meaning the element will be dropped). If it is not in the set, we add it to it and return `true`, so the element will be included in the resulting array.

3. Go to `SetTests.swift`, uncomment the unit test, and run it.

Dictionaries

A `Dictionary` is an *unordered* collection of mappings/associations from keys to values. It is very similar to a Set and has the same performance, but stores a key/value pair, and only the key has to be `Hashable`. It can be used for storing preferences, or when you have a group of named values that are either too many or change too often to be hardcoded. Then, you can use the names as keys.

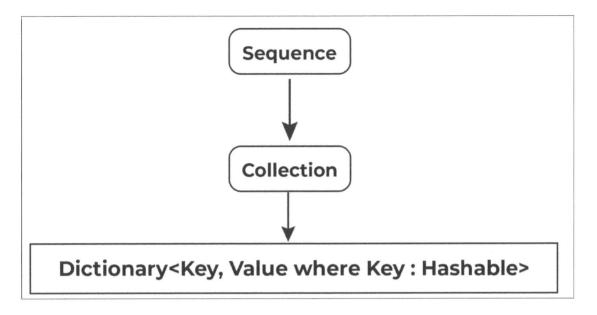

The full name is `Dictionary<Key, Value>`, but it is more commonly written as `[Key:
Value]`.

Dictionary ignores the order in which values are added or removed, and may change it
arbitrarily, just like Set.

Working with Dictionaries

Here are a few basic operations with dictionaries:

1. Create a dictionary and print it to observe that the order is not preserved:

```
var numbers = [0: "zero", 1: "one", 10: "ten", 100: "one
hundred"]
print(numbers) // [100: "one hundred", 10: "ten", 0: "zero", 1:
"one"]
```

2. Add or change a value:

```
numbers[20] = "twenty" // sets value "twenty" for key 20.
```

3. Lookups return optionals:

```
if let one = numbers[1] {
    // ...
}
```

Or you can use a default value if the key is not found:

```
let two = numbers[2, default: "no sensible default"]
```

4. Remove a value by setting it to nil:

```
numbers[2] = nil
```

5. Iterate over the contents of the dictionary (the order is not defined):

```
for (key, value) in numbers {
    // ...
}
```

6. Access the keys and values separately:

```
numbers.keys // A collection of all keys
numbers.values // A collection of all values
```

7. Run the code. This is what will appear on your screen:

```
var numbers = [0: "zero", 1: "one", 10: "ten", 100: "one        [100: "one hundred", 1: "one", 0: "zero", 10: "ten"]
    hundred"]
print(numbers)                                                   "[100: "one hundred", 1: "one", 0: "zero", 10: "ten"]\n"

numbers[20] = "twenty" // Add or change value                    "twenty"

// Look up returns an optional
if let one = numbers[1] {
    one                                                          "one"
}

// Or you can use a default value if the key is not found
let two = numbers[2, default: "no sensible default"]             "no sensible default"

// Remove a value by setting it to nil
numbers[2] = nil                                                 nil

// You can iterate over the contents (again: order is not
    defined)
for (key, value) in numbers {
    key                                                          (5 times)
    value                                                        (5 times)
}

// A collection of all keys
numbers.keys                                                     Dictionary.Keys([100, 1, 20, 0, 10])

// A collection of all values
numbers.values                                                   Dictionary.Values(["one hundred", "one", "twenty", "zer...
```

```
[100: "one hundred", 1: "one", 0: "zero", 10: "ten"]
```

Activity: Using Dictionaries

A CountedSet allows you to add equal elements more than once, and keeps count of how many of each element it contains. Naturally, it is very useful for counting things, such as how many times a word appears in a text, without having to store each word more than once.

We will develop the new CountedSet type using a dictionary internally.

1. Open the CollectionsExtra Xcode project we used earlier, and go to CountedSet. swift.

2. Leave the commented-out code as is, and add this to the top of the file:

```
public struct CountedSet<Element: Hashable> {
  typealias ElementsDictionary = [Element: Int]
  private var elements: ElementsDictionary

  public init() {
    elements = ElementsDictionary()
  }
}
```

We use a type alias here because `ElementsDictionary` will be referred to several times in the code.

3. Add the following code below the initialiser:

```
public mutating func insert(_ newelement: Element, count: Int = 1) {
  elements[newelement, default: 0] += count
}
```

When inserting, we first get the current count of the element (or 0 if the element is not in the dictionary), then we add how many times the element should be inserted (1 by default) to this and insert the new value into the dictionary. `+=` here means this:

```
elements[newelement] = elements[newelement, default: 0] + count
```

4. Now, we implement adding a `Sequence` of elements to the set:

```
public mutating func insert<S>(contentsOf other: S) where S:Sequence,
S.Element == Element {
  for newelement in other {
    insert(newelement)
  }
}
```

The generic `<S>` combined with the `where` clause allows us to use any sequence here, as long as its elements are the same type as the elements of this set.

5. We also need a way to query how many of an element this set contains:

```
public func count(for element: Element) -> Int {
   return elements[element, default: 0]
}
```

If the `elements` dictionary does not contain the element, we return 0 instead.

6. And here is the method for counting the total number of elements:

```
public var count: Int {
   var result = 0
   for count in elements.values {
      result += count
   }
   return result
}
```

7. It's time to check if this is working. Go to `CountedSetTests.swift`, uncomment the `testInsert` unit test, and run it.

8. Go back to `CountedSet.swift`.

9. Now, we can add some helpful initialisers. Add the following code below the first initialiser:

```
public init<S>(_ other: S) where S:Sequence, S.Element == Element {
   self.init()
   insert(contentsOf: other)
}
```

This allows us to initialise from a sequence:

```
CountedSet(["a","b","c","a"])
```

10. Add the following code below the entire struct declaration:

```
extension CountedSet: ExpressibleByArrayLiteral {
   public init(arrayLiteral elementarray: Element...) {
      self.init(elementarray)
   }
}
```

Now, if a function asks for a `CountedSet`, we can use an array literal directly.

11. Within the struct declaration, right below the last `count` method, insert the following code:

```
@discardableResult
public mutating func remove(_ element: Element, count countToRemove: Int
= 1) -> Int {
  guard var count = elements[element] else { return 0 }
  count -= countToRemove
  guard count > 0 else {
    elements.removeValue(forKey: element)
    return 0
  }
  elements[element] = count
  return count
}
```

This is the most complex code we have used so far. It lowers the count of the element by the provided amount, and returns the new count.

- ° `@discardableResult` means if we do not use the return value from this method, we don't want a warning from the compiler.

- ° We retrieve the current count of the element. If it is not in the dictionary, we return `0`.

- ° Then, we subtract with the provided amount.

- ° If the new count is not greater than `0`, we remove the element from the dictionary and return `0`.

- ° Otherwise, we store the new count in the dictionary and return it.

12. At the bottom of the file, there is code for adopting the `Collection` protocol. Uncomment it. It is too long to go through in detail here, but feel free to look through it.

13. Also uncomment all the unit tests in `CountedSetTests.swift`, and verify that they all pass. Notice how the unit tests use methods such as `contains` and `isEmpty` that we did not implement, but got for free because we adopted the `Collection` protocol.

14. The `contains` method from the collection protocol is quite inefficient for our type, because it goes through every single element and compares it to the element it is searching for. We can do better. Add the following code below the `remove` method in the struct declaration:

```
public func contains(_ element: Element) -> Bool {
    return elements[element] != nil
}
```

This checks the dictionary directly, which as we mentioned earlier is much faster.

Summary

In this lesson, we covered the three main collections in the Swift Standard Library: Array, Set, and Dictionary; what they are; and how they can be used. We learned about indices, slices/subsequences, and some common protocols. We implemented methods for searching in sorted arrays, for removing duplicates from a sequence, and created the new collection, `CountedSet`.

In the next lesson, we will explore Strings in detail.

5

Strings

The wide variety of characters and emojis a modern app may encounter requires correct handling of Unicode text. Luckily, Swift does this by default. This means we have to treat strings in Swift a bit differently than most programming languages.

Lesson Objectives

By the end of this lesson, you will be able to:

- Explain why strings work the way they do in Swift
- Create and use strings and substrings
- Perform common string operations

String Fundamentals

Before we get into how to use strings, we will cover why they are the way they are. Because for developers coming from other languages, this is a very reasonable question to ask.

Character

We won't go into the details of Unicode, but there are several ways of viewing a piece of Unicode text in Swift. This is done by using different collections:

```
let string = "The ☀ and ☽"
string.utf8.count // 19
string.utf16.count // 13
string.unicodeScalars.count // 12
```

 An element of UTF-8 is 1 byte, UTF-16 is 2 bytes, and a Unicode scalar is 4 bytes.

In addition to everyone reporting a different number of symbols in the string, you may have also noticed that they are all wrong. `String` itself, however, has the right answer:

```
string.count // 11
```

This is because `String` is an ordered collection of `Character`. `Character` represents what we humans would consider *one* symbol, regardless of how many bytes it consists of.

The reason for the discrepancies is, of course, the two emojis:

```
let moon = Character("☽")
String(moon).utf8.count // 4
String(moon).utf16.count // 2
moon.unicodeScalars.count // 1

let sun: Character = "☀"
String(sun).utf8.count // 6
String(sun).utf16.count // 2
sun.unicodeScalars.count // 2
```

Even a simple letter like é may surprise you:

```
let accented_e: Character = "é"
String(accented_e).utf8.count // 2
String(accented_e).utf16.count // 1
accented_e.unicodeScalars.count // 1
```

There may be several ways of representing the same symbol in Unicode, but `Character` still considers them to be equal:

```
let another_accented_e: Character = "e\u{0301}" // "e" + combining acute
accent
String(another_accented_e).utf8.count // 3
String(another_accented_e).utf16.count // 2
another_accented_e.unicodeScalars.count // 2

accented_e == another_accented_e // true
```

 This is a great example of two values that are equal, but not identical.

Collection

Let's see what kind of a collection `String` is:

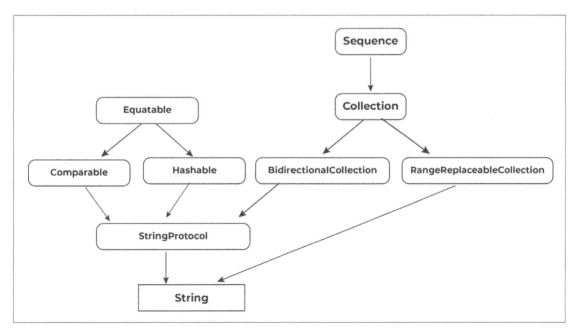

`StringProtocol` contains common string operations.

Comparing this diagram with the one for `Array` in the *Working with Arrays* section of the previous lesson, we see that both `MutableCollection` and `RandomAccessCollection` are missing.

This is because, as we have seen, symbols may take up varying amounts of space, and in a `MutableCollection`, we can replace one element for another. But what if we replace one character with one that takes more space? Then we would have to move all succeeding characters to make room, and the `MutableCollection` protocol does not allow this. It is the same with `RandomAccessCollection`: it requires taking approximately the same amount of time to retrieve the 5th element as the 20,000th, and we can't do that when the elements are not of the same size.

So, why not add some padding and make all characters in a string take up the same amount of memory? Well, we did have an array of characters in the previous lesson, which does just that. Let's bring it back and compare its memory usage with the corresponding string:

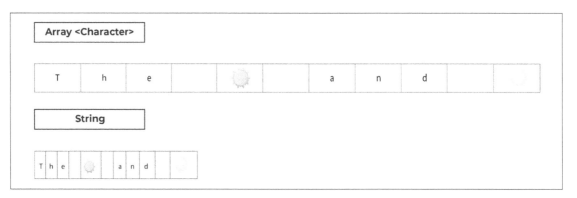

An instance of `Character` takes up eight bytes in an array. The most common characters usually take up two bytes or fewer in a string, and as strings are often the largest collections in an application, wasting all that space is not really an option.

Index

Just like arrays, strings have indices, which refer to the position of every single character. But before we get into what the type of String's index is, we should cover what it is *not*: an integer.

The index type of an *array* is an integer. Because every element takes up the same amount of space, you can ask for the 500th element and it will multiply 500 with the byte size of an element, add the memory address of the first element, and find the element at the resulting address.

If we ask a *string* for the 500th character, it has to start with the first character, see how much space it takes, move past it, see how much space the next character takes, and so on, and repeat this 500 times.

On StackOverflow and other places, you will often find code examples which add a new subscript to String with an integer parameter, allowing us to do something like this:

```
for i in 0..<string.count {
  let character = string[i]
  // ...
}
```

This is extremely inefficient. Consider what is actually happening here: the string has to process the first character, then the first and second characters, then the first, second, and third characters, and so on. For a string of merely 500 characters, it will have processed the first character 500 times, the second one 499, and so on until it has processed characters $n(n+1)/2$ or 125,250 times, plus 500 to find the count.

The following, however, will visit each character exactly once, and is much simpler:

```
for character in string {
  // ...
}
```

Working with String Index

The actual index type of `String` is `String.Index`. It's a custom type whose inner workings we are blissfully unaware of. All operations on it are performed using the standard `Collection` and `BidirectionalCollection` methods on `String`.

- Define a few indices:

```
let alphabet = "abcdefghijklmnopqrstuvwxyz"

let b_index = alphabet.index(after: alphabet.startIndex)
let a_index = alphabet.index(before: b_index)
let g_index = alphabet.index(a_index, offsetBy: 6)
let e_index = alphabet.index(g_index, offsetBy: -2)
```

- We can also add a limit to the offset. We get `nil` if the result goes beyond this limit:

```
let no_index = alphabet.index(e_index, offsetBy: 30, limitedBy:
alphabet.endIndex)
```

- Here is how to find the index of the first occurrence of a character (we get `nil` if it is not found):

```
let i = alphabet.index(of: "z")
```

- And the number of positions one index is from another:

```
let a_e_distance = alphabet.distance(from: a_index, to: e_index)
```

Debugging

Perhaps the biggest drawback of using this custom type instead of an integer comes up during debugging, when we would like to see what it contains. If we just print an index to the console, we get something like this:

```
Swift.String.Index(_compoundOffset: 100, _cache: Swift.String.Index._Cache.
character(1))
```

This contains nothing of interest. If we add this extension in a unit test module, we get something more useful:

```
// use in unit tests
extension String.Index: CustomDebugStringConvertible {
  // The offset into a string's UTF-16 encoding for this index.
  public var debugDescription: String { return "\(encodedOffset)" }
}
```

Now, when we print an index, we get the zero-based position of this index in the string *if this string, so far, only contains characters that can be expressed in one UTF-16 code unit*. So it's not always correct, but better than nothing.

Activity: All Indices of a Character

The `String.index(of:)` method finds the index of the first occurrence of a character in a string. In this activity, we'll create a method which finds all the indices of a character.

1. Open the `StringsExtra` Xcode project, and go to the `StringsExtra.swift` file.
2. Enter the following code:

    ```
    extension String {
    ```

    ○ The method definition is similar to the one for `index(of:)`:

    ```
    public func indices(of character: Character) -> [Index] {
        var result = [Index]()
        var i = startIndex
    ```

    ○ Make sure to not access anything at `endIndex`, as it will crash. This check also takes care of empty strings:

    ```
    while i < endIndex {
        if self[i] == character {
            result.append(i)
        }
    ```

    ○ Move to the next index:

    ```
            i = index(after: i)
        }
        return result
        }
    }
    ```

This is the traditional way of implementing it, to show how to work directly with indices. Later, we will learn a much simpler and concise way of doing this.

3. Go to the unit tests in `StringsExtraTests.swift`.

4. Uncomment the first comment block, so this becomes active:

   ```
   func testIndices()
   ```

5. Run the unit test and verify that it passes.

Using Strings

So far in this course we have only covered the Swift Standard Library, but when it comes to strings we must also include the Foundation framework, as it contains a lot of both basic and advanced text functionality that is missing from the Swift Standard Library.

Foundation is available on all Apple platforms and has been around for a long time (there is also a version for other platforms, re-implemented in Swift; see: `https://github.com/apple/swift-corelibs-foundation`). It is written in and for Objective-C, but a lot of its API has been updated to be easier to work with from Swift. Not all of it has been though, and as we'll see, you might run into some problems when converting Foundation types to Swift types.

Foundation's string type is `NSString`, and it works directly with UTF-16 encoded text. It does not know what the Character type is, and does not necessarily handle Unicode text correctly like Swift does. `NSString` can be used as Swift String and vice versa as they can share the same underlying storage.

It also has `CharacterSet`, which, despite the name, is a set of `UnicodeScalar`. It has several useful predefined sets, like `CharacterSet.alphanumerics`, `.whitespaces`, `.decimalDigits`, and more. You can only use them if you're lucky enough to have characters consisting of only one `UnicodeScalar`:

```
CharacterSet.alphanumerics.contains(character.unicodeScalars.first!)
```

Foundation's range type is `NSRange`, and it uses integers to refer to positions in an `NSString`. It can do this efficiently because each element of `NSString` takes up the same amount of space. We can always convert a Swift Range to NSRange with `NSRange(range, in: string)`, but we can't necessarily go the other way, as we will see later on.

Creating Strings

There are many ways of creating strings:

- You've already seen the string literal:

```
let literal = "string from literal"
```

- There are also multi-line literals:

```
let multilineLiteral = """
  line 1
  line 2
    line 3 indented

  """
```

The result is `"line 1\nline 2\n\tline 3 indented\n"`. The closing three quotes must be at the beginning of the line (excluding indentation) and any indentation that precedes it will be removed from the beginning of every line in the string.

- Use backslash to insert special characters like \\ (backslash), \t (horizontal tab), \n (line feed), \r (carriage return), \" (double quotation mark), and \' (single quotation mark).

- We can create characters directly from their hexadecimal Unicode code points:

```
let blackDiamond = "\u{2666}" // ♦
let brokenHeart = "\u{1F494}" // 💔
```

- To include variables in the text, we use string interpolation:

```
let array = [1,2,3]
let stringInterpolation = "The array \(array) has \(array.count) items."
// "The array [1, 2, 3] has 3 items."
```

- Strings can describe absolutely any type:

```
struct CustomType {
  let value: Int
  let otherValue: Bool
}

let customType = CustomType(value: 5, otherValue: false)
String(describing: customType) // "CustomType(value: 5, otherValue:
false)"
```

- We can customize the description:

```
extension CustomType: CustomStringConvertible {
  var description: String {
    return "\(value) and \(otherValue)"
  }
}

String(describing: customType) // "5 and false"
```

- Text can be repeated:

```
String(repeating: "la", count: 5)
```

- We can read text files:

```
import Foundation

do {
  let fileContents = try String(contentsOfFile: "file.txt")
} catch { /* ... */ }
```

Common Operations

Here are some common text operations:

- Many of the common sequence and collection methods are useful on strings too:

```
let string = """
          Line 1
          line 2
          """
let range1 = ..<string.index(of: "1")!

// return the substring over range 1
```

```
string[range1]

// return true if the string begins with "Line"
string.hasPrefix("Line")
// return true if the string ends with "2"
string.hasSuffix("2")
```

- These mutate the string:

```
var mutablestring = string

// remove the characters in range1, and insert "line up" there.
mutablestring.replaceSubrange(range1, with: "line up")
// remove the characters in range1.
mutablestring.removeSubrange(range1)
// remove the first character.
mutablestring.removeFirst()
// remove the first 2 characters.
mutablestring.removeFirst(2)
// remove the last character.
mutablestring.removeLast()
// remove the last 2 characters.
mutablestring.removeLast(2)
```

- These are operations specifically made for strings:

```
// return a new string in uppercase.
string.uppercased()
// return a new string in lowercase.
string.lowercased()
```

- We get a lot more if we import Foundation, like this simple test for the existence of a substring:

```
string.contains(" 1")
```

- All of the following methods return a new string with the changes; the original string is left intact:

```
// new string with all the words capitalised (ignoring language)
string.capitalized
// new string with all the words capitalised, using the rules of the
language from the provided locale
string.capitalized(with: Locale.current)
// new string with all occurrences of one substring replaced with
another
string.replacingOccurrences(of: "Line", with: "line")
// new string with all occurrences of a substring removed
string.replacingOccurrences(of: "Line", with: "")
// new string with all occurrences of a substring in the provided range
removed, using the provided options
string.replacingOccurrences(of: "line", with: "triangle", options:
.caseInsensitive, range: string.startIndex..<string.index(of: "\n")!)


// the range of the first character that belongs to the provided
CharacterSet
string.rangeOfCharacter(from: .decimalDigits)
// the range of the first occurrence of the substring
let range = string.range(of: "Line")!
// the substring over this range
string[range]
// the range of the line or lines containing the provided range
string.lineRange(for: range)
// new string with the characters in the provided CharacterSet removed
from the beginning and the end
" \t  trim  \n ".trimmingCharacters(in: .whitespacesAndNewlines)
// a new string of the given length, by either removing characters from
the end or adding 'withPad' to the end
"Padded".padding(toLength: 10, withPad: " ", startingAt: 0)
"Pad".padding(toLength: 10, withPad: "_ ", startingAt: 1)
```

- The following methods return an array of strings:

```
// an array of strings, from splitting the original string over the
provided substring
string.components(separatedBy: ". ")
// an array of strings, from splitting the original string over
characters in the provided CharacterSet
string.components(separatedBy: .newlines)
```

Activity: All Ranges of a Substring

There is already a method on String for finding the first range of a substring. This method will find all of the ranges of a substring.

1. Open the `StringsExtra` Xcode project, and go to the StringsExtra.swift file.

2. Enter the following code:

```
import Foundation

extension String {
```

° The method has the same parameters as `String.range`:

```
public func allRanges(of aString: String,
    options: String.CompareOptions = [],
    range searchRange: Range<String.Index>? = nil,
    locale: Locale? = nil) -> [Range<String.Index>] {
```

° If no search range is given, we search the entire string:

```
var searchRange = searchRange ?? startIndex..<endIndex
var ranges = [Range<String.Index>]()
```

° `while let` is a very useful combination of loop and optionals. It continues until `self.range` returns `nil`:

```
while let foundRange = self.range(of: aString, options: options,
range: searchRange, locale: locale) {
    ranges.append(foundRange)
```

If we are searching backwards, we need to narrow the search range from the right instead of from the left. We only narrow it by one character so we can find repeating substrings (like the five occurrences of `lala` in `lalalalalala`):

```
searchRange = options.contains(.backwards) ?
    searchRange.lowerBound..<self.index(before: foundRange.
upperBound) :
    self.index(after: foundRange.lowerBound)..<searchRange.
upperBound
    }
    return ranges
  }
}
```

3. Go to the unit tests in `StringsExtraTests.swift`.

4. Uncomment the first comment block, so these become active:

```
let string = """
func testAllRanges()
```

5. Run all unit tests and verify that they pass.

Activity: Counting Words, Sentences, and Paragraphs

Perhaps the most straightforward way of counting the number of words in a string is to count the number of spaces and add one. But, even if you only have text using the Latin alphabet, this will often be wrong (there could be two spaces in a row, and "doesn't" is technically two words). Foundation has `NSLinguisticTagger`, which handles these things and other alphabets. Not all of its APIs have been updated for Swift yet, so it can be a bit cumbersome to use, but the method that we will use here is fairly straightforward.

1. Open the `StringsExtra` Xcode project, and go to the `StringsExtra.swift` file.

2. Enter the following code:

```
extension String {
```

   ° `NSLinguisticTaggerUnit` is an enum with cases `paragraph`, `sentence`, and `word`:

```
public func countLinguisticTokens(ofType unit: NSLinguisticTaggerUnit,
options: NSLinguisticTagger.Options = [.omitPunctuation,
.omitWhitespace]) -> Int {
```

   ° This class can do a lot of advanced text analysis, such as detecting nouns, verbs, and so on, and find the stem of words, but in this case we are only interested in *linguistic tokens*:

```
let tagger = NSLinguisticTagger(tagSchemes: [.tokenType], options:
0)

tagger.string = self
```

- ○ Like everything in Foundation, this class works on NSString, which sometimes uses NSRange instead of Range. Luckily, converting from Range to NSRange is no problem:

```
let range = NSRange(startIndex..<endIndex, in: self)
var result = 0
```

This closure has parameters for a tag type, nsrange, and a Boolean for whether or not it should stop, but in this case we are only interested in how many times it is called:

```
    tagger.enumerateTags(in: range, unit: unit, scheme: .tokenType,
options: options, using: { _, _, _ in
        result += 1
    })
    return result
  }
}
```

3. You can call it like this:

```
string.countLinguisticTokens(ofType: .paragraph)
string.countLinguisticTokens(ofType: .sentence)
string.countLinguisticTokens(ofType: .word)
```

4. Go to the unit tests in StringsExtraTests.swift.

5. Uncomment the next comment block, so these become active:

```
let english = """
func testCountLinguisticTokens_English() {
let internationalText = """
func testCountLinguisticTokens_International() {
```

6. Run all unit tests and verify that they pass.

Substring

SubString is for strings what ArraySlice is for arrays: a view of a part of a string, where its startIndex and endIndex are indices into the original string. It conforms to the same protocols as String:

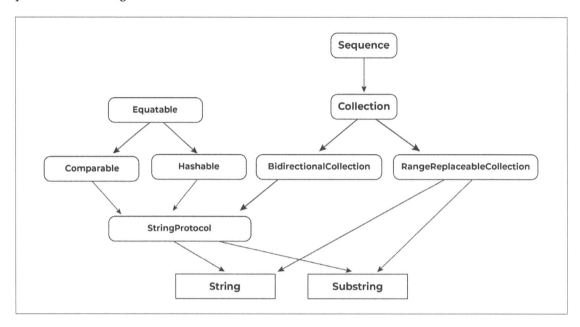

StringProtocol contains many of the common text operations, so when you write functions that take a string parameter you can often use StringProtocol instead to also accept substrings. When you do, you have to use generics, as shown here:

```
func foo<S: StringProtocol>(s: S) {
    // use 's' almost like a normal string.
}
```

Just as with ArraySlice, substrings keep a reference to the entire string, so when you are done processing substrings you should turn them into normal strings and allow the original string to be released (if nothing else is using it):

```
String(substring)
```

Creating Substrings

Substrings can be created in many different ways:

- We can create substrings by passing a range of indices to a string subscript:
  ```
  string[from..<upTo]
  string[from...upToAndIncluding]
  ```

- And we get a substring of the entire string with this little shortcut:
  ```
  string[...]
  ```

- The following methods return a substring and leave the original string intact:
  ```
  let string = "This is  a pretty 👆 sentence"

  // a substring from the 2nd character and out
  string.dropFirst()
  // a substring from the 6th character and out
  string.dropFirst(5)
  // a substring from the first up to and including the second last
  string.dropLast()
  // a substring from the first up to the 9th last character
  string.dropLast(9)
  // a substring from the first space and out
  string.drop(while: {$0 != " "})

  // the index of the first space, or the first character if there are no
  spaces
  let space_index = string.index(of: " ") ?? string.startIndex
  // a substring with the first 7 characters
  string.prefix(7)
  // a substring from the first up to space_index (excluding)
  string.prefix(upTo: space_index)
  // a substring from the first up to and including space_index
  string.prefix(through: space_index)
  // a substring of the consonants at the beginning of the string ("Th")
  string.prefix(while: {![ "a", "e", "i", "o", "u"].contains($0)})
  // a substring of the last 8 characters
  string.suffix(8)
  // a substring from space_index and out
  string.suffix(from: space_index)
  ```

- While these return an array of substrings:

```
// the substrings between the spaces
string.split(separator: " ")
// split the string into 5 substrings (at the first 4 spaces), including
the empty substring between the 2 adjacent spaces
string.split(separator: " ", maxSplits: 4, omittingEmptySubsequences:
false)
// the substrings between the vowels
string.split(whereSeparator: {["a", "e", "i", "o", "u"].contains($0)})
```

Parsing Strings

These different ways of creating substrings are very useful for extracting parts of text. Try it yourself in this little example:

1. Go to the `Exercise - Parse` page of the `Strings` playground. Enter the code to turn this:

```
let info = """
   title: Beginning Swift
   type: course
   year: 2018
   publisher: Packt Publishing
   topic: programming
   """
```

Into this dictionary:

```
["year": "2018", "publisher": "Packt Publishing", "title": "Beginning
Swift", "topic": "programming", "type": "course"]
```

2. Here is one possible solution:

```
var result = [String: String]()
for line in info.split(separator: "\n") {
  guard let colon = line.index(of: ":") else { continue }
  let key = line.prefix(upTo: colon)
  let value = line.suffix(from: line.index(colon, offsetBy: 2))
  result[String(key)] = String(value)
}
```

Converting NSRange to Range

Earlier, we made the countLinguisticTokens method for counting the number of words, sentences, and paragraphs in a string. It would be nice if we could get hold of the actual words, sentences, and paragraphs, too:

```
func linguisticTokens(ofType unit: NSLinguisticTaggerUnit, options:
NSLinguisticTagger.Options = [.omitPunctuation, .omitWhitespace]) ->
[String] {
  let tagger = NSLinguisticTagger(tagSchemes: [.tokenType], options: 0)
  tagger.string = self
  let range = NSRange(startIndex..<endIndex, in: self)
  var result = [String]()
  tagger.enumerateTags(in: range, unit: unit, scheme: .tokenType, options:
options, using: { _, tokenRange, _ in
    let token = (self as NSString).substring(with: tokenRange)
    result.append(token)
  })
  return result
}
```

The only changes are the return type and these two lines:

```
    let token = (self as NSString).substring(with: tokenRange)
    result.append(token)
```

tokenRange is of type NSRange, so we can't use it directly on String, but have to cast ourselves into NSString first.

This works fine, but it would be even nicer and more *Swifty* if we could get back ranges instead of strings, so we can decide for ourselves if we want to turn them into substrings or strings or do other operations with them. See attempts of this in the Failed linguisticTokens return Range page of Strings.playground. If we try to convert the NSRange to a Swift Range with Range(tokenRange, in: self), it returns an optional, and worse, in the third-last line of the example text, it returns nil. Twice. This is presumably because these characters do not fit in one UTF-16 code unit, and the conversion would create an index pointing to the middle of a Swift Character (see methods linguisticTokens2 and linguisticTokens3 for attempts at moving the index to the correct side of this character).

This highlights the usefulness of a string type which takes care of these things for us, and potential problems with converting between Foundation types and Swift types, not to mention the importance of testing with various languages.

Luckily, there is another Foundation method we can use that returns Swift ranges. We will use `enumerateLinguisticTags` in the next activity.

Activity: CamelCase

Create a method on String which returns itself as one CamelCased word, optionally with the first letter lowercased.

This can be used to automatically format code or create a text service on the Mac.

1. Open the `StringsExtra` Xcode project, and go to the `StringsExtra.swift` file.

2. Add this code to the bottom of the file:

```
extension String {
```

   ° First, we create a method which returns an array of ranges of all the words in the string:

```
public func wordRanges() -> [Range<String.Index>] {
    let options: NSLinguisticTagger.Options = [.omitPunctuation,
.omitWhitespace]
    var words = [Range<String.Index>]()
```

   ° This method on String gives us Swift ranges (as opposed to the NSRanges of the `linguisticTokens` method we used previously). Unfortunately, it doesn't provide sentences or paragraphs, but in this case words are all we need:

```
self.enumerateLinguisticTags(
    in: startIndex..<endIndex,
    scheme: NSLinguisticTagScheme.tokenType.rawValue,
    options: options) { (_, range, _, _) in
        words.append(range)
    }
    return words
}
```

- ° Now for the `camelCased` method itself, which returns a capitalised CamelCase word by default:

```
public func camelCased(capitalised: Bool = true) -> String {
```

  - ° First, we get all the ranges of the words in this string. We exit if there are no words in order to avoid a crash in the next line (`removeFirst` removes and returns the first element, and crashes if there isn't one):

```
var wordRanges = self.wordRanges()
guard !wordRanges.isEmpty else { return "" }
let firstRange = wordRanges.removeFirst()
```

  - ° We initialize `result` to the first word, which is optionally capitalised. Note that both `capitalized` and `lowercased` are methods on SubString which return strings:

```
var result = capitalised ? self[firstRange].capitalized :
self[firstRange].lowercased()
```

Then, it's a simple matter of going through the remaining words, capitalizing them, and adding them to `result`:

```
    for range in wordRanges {
        result += self[range].capitalized
    }
    return result
  }
}
```

3. Go to the unit tests in `StringsExtraTests.swift`.

4. Uncomment the next comment block, so this becomes active:

```
func testCamelCased() {
```

5. Run all unit tests and verify that they pass.

Summary

In this lesson, we learned about strings in Swift, how they are and why, and how to use them. We learned about string indices, substrings, and some things to look out for when using strings with the Foundation framework. And we added some useful extensions to `String`.

In the next lesson, we will take a brief look at functional programming and explore lazy operations.

6

Functional Programming and Lazy Operations

In this lesson, we will take a brief look at functional programming and learn what lazy operations are. We will end with an important but often overlooked topic: writing Swifty code.

Functional programming is a style of programming which tries to keep things simple by avoiding state, especially mutable state, and using a relatively small set of highly versatile functions/methods which take other functions as input. The Swift Standard Library contains several of these. They often make the code shorter, simpler, and easier to read if you know what they do. They can also free you from the burden of having to come up with names for temporary variables. Even if you don't use them in your own code, it is important to know how they work as a lot of Swift code out there uses them.

Lesson Objectives

By the end of this lesson, you will be able to:

- Use the `filter`, `map`/`forEach`, `flatMap`, and `reduce` methods
- Use lazy sequences to delay operations until they are needed
- Write proper *Swifty* code

Function Type

 Open `Functional.playground` at the `Introduction` page.

First, let's reiterate what a function type is:

```
var sum: (Int, Int) -> Int
```

The type of `sum` is a function that takes two `Int` values and returns one `Int` value. We can assign both functions and closures to it, as they are essentially the same thing:

```
func sumFunction(a: Int, b: Int) -> Int {
   return a + b
}
let sumClosure = {(a: Int, b: Int) in return a + b}

sum = sumFunction
sum = sumClosure
```

We can also assign an operator to it:

```
sum = (+)
```

This is because an operator is a function (the parentheses around the + operator are just to signal that we want to use it as a function, not add things together right away). The definition of the + operator for `Int` is:

```
static func +(lhs: Int, rhs: Int) -> Int
```

So whenever a function has a parameter of a function type, we can supply an operator, as long as the input and output match:

```
func perform(operation: (Int, Int) -> Int, on a: Int, _ b: Int) -> Int {
   return operation(a,b)
}

perform(operation: +, on: 1, 2)
```

Initialisers can also be used as functions:

```
extension Int {
  init(add a: Int, _ b: Int) {
    self.init(a + b)
```

```
    }
}

sum = Int.init
perform(operation: Int.init, on: 2, 3)
```

We have to use `.init` to show that we are referring to an initialiser, not the type `Int` itself.

If several functions have the same name, or initialisers have the same number and types of arguments, we can specify which one we are referring to by including the argument labels. Here are the full names of the preceding functions:

```
sumFunction(a:b:)
perform(operation:on:_:)
Int.init(add:_:)
```

Functional Methods

 Open `Functional.playground` at the `Methods` page.

 The following sections show different ways of performing the same tasks. They say nothing about which version is better.

filter

The `filter` method looks like this:

```
func filter(_ isIncluded: (Element) throws -> Bool) rethrows -> [Element]
```

It is a simple method on `Sequence`, and we have already used it. The input function takes an element of the sequence and returns either `false` or `true`. `filter` returns an array of only those elements for which the input function returns `true`:

```
let numbers = [-4,4,2,-8,0]
let negative = numbers.filter {$0<0} // [-4, -8]
```

`Set` and `Dictionary` have their own versions of this method, which return a Set or Dictionary respectively.

Using the filter Method

It is often simpler to use an existing collection that has everything we want, and filter it, than creating an empty collection and adding what we want. Let's do that here:

1. In *Activity A: All Indices of a Character* of *Lesson 5, Strings*, we implemented a method on String for finding the indices of all occurrences of a character. Go to the Exercise - filter page in Functional.playground and replace the body of the method with one that uses filter. Make sure the unit test passes afterwards.

Here's a hint: when introducing arrays in *Lesson 4*, we mentioned how to get all the indices of a collection.

Here's the solution:

```
return indices.filter { self[$0] == character }
```

map

map is a method often used on container types. For Sequence, it looks like this:

```
func map<T>(_ transform: (Element) throws -> T) rethrows -> [T]
```

Each element of the sequence is passed to the input function, and the outputs are returned in an array. This is a straight one-to-one transformation, where the resulting array has the same number of elements as the sequence.

map is remarkably versatile. Once you know about it, you'll be seeing uses for it everywhere. Here's how we can use it to perform mathematical operations on arrays of numbers:

```
let numbers = [-4,4,2,-8,0]
let squared = numbers.map {$0*$0} // [16, 16, 4, 64, 0]
```

There is also a similar function on Sequence that doesn't return anything:

```
func forEach(_ body: (Element) throws -> Void) rethrows
```

This does the exact same thing as map, except it doesn't return an array, because the input function doesn't return anything. It avoids having to create and return an array of Void (even Void takes up space in an array):

```
squared.forEach { print($0) }
```

Perhaps surprisingly, we also have `map` on optionals. This makes sense if you think of an optional as a container of either 0 or 1 elements:

```
func map<U>(_ transform: (Element) throws -> U) rethrows -> U?
```

If the optional is `nil`, map returns `nil`. If not, the value the optional contains is passed to the input function, and the result is returned in an optional.

This is very useful for initialisers and other functions which return optionals, such as `Int(String)`, which can only create an integer if the string contains one:

```
let textTimesTwo = Int("4").map { $0 * 2 }
```

Or, if we have an optional delegate we want to pass to a function, but only if it is not `nil`. Here is the obvious way of doing it:

```
if let delegate = delegate {
   doSomething(with: delegate)
}
```

Using `map` is shorter and more to the point:

```
delegate.map(doSomething)
```

Using the map Method

Try for yourself to use both the sequence map and the optional version:

1. Go to the `Exercise - map` page in `Functional.playground`.

2. Create an array with the number of characters of each word in `text`.

3. Edit the body of the `range(where predicate: (Element) throws -> Bool)` method to use the optional `map` instead of `guard let`.

Solution to 2:

```
let wordLengths = text.split(separator: " ").map {$0.count}
```

Solution to 3:

```
return try index(where: predicate).map { start in
  let end = try self[start..<endIndex]
    .index(where: { try !predicate($0) }) ?? endIndex
  return start..<end
}
```

flatMap

What if the function you provide to `map` returns an array, and you don't want to end up with an array of arrays? The `flatMap` method on `Sequence` takes care of that:

```
func flatMap<S:Sequence>(_ transform: (Element) throws -> S) rethrows ->
[S.Element]
```

The input function takes an element and returns a sequence of elements, possibly of another type. `flatMap` runs the input function on each of the original sequence's elements, joins the resulting sequences together, and returns them in an array. You can think of it as first running a normal `map`, then flattening the resulting sequence of sequences into a normal sequence.

Here's how you can use it to split up an array of ranges into a single array of bounds:

```
let ranges = [0...2, 5...7, 10...11]
let bounds = ranges.flatMap { [$0.lowerBound, $0.upperBound] }
// [0, 2, 5, 7, 10, 11]
```

There is also a slightly different method of the same name on `Sequence`:

```
func flatMap<U>(_ transform: (Element) throws -> U?) rethrows -> [U]
```

Here, the input function returns an optional, even if the sequence does not contain optionals. Every time the input function returns `nil`, it is ignored. This is more like a combination of `map` and then filtering out all `nil` values. The method is misnamed, and will be renamed to `compactMap` (https://github.com/apple/swift-evolution/blob/master/proposals/0187-introduce-filtermap.md) in Swift 4.1:

```
["a","1","b","3"].flatMap(Int.init) // [1, 3]
```

Optional has its own version of `flatMap`:

```
func flatMap<U>(_ transform: (Element) throws -> U?) rethrows -> U?
```

If the optional is `nil`, `flatMap` returns `nil`. Otherwise, the value the optional contains is passed to the input function, and the result is returned. Using this function instead of `map` avoids getting an optional of an optional in return:

```
var stringOptional: String?
...
let intOptional = stringOptional.flatMap(Int.init)
```

Using the flatMap Method

Try out `flatMap` for yourself:

1. Go to the `Exercise - flatMap` page in `Functional.playground`.

2. Create the inverted array using one `flatMap` instead of a `filter` and a `map`.

3. Change the body of the `range(between:and:)` function to use `flatMap` and `map` instead of `guard let`.

Solution to 2:

```
let inverted = numbers.flatMap { nr in
  return nr == 0 ? [] : [1.0/Double(nr)]
}
```

Or:

```
let inverted = numbers.flatMap { nr in
  return nr == 0 ? nil : 1.0/Double(nr)
}
```

Solution to 3:

```
public func range(between fromElement: Element, and toElement: Element) ->
Range<Index>? {
  return index(of: fromElement)
    .flatMap { fromIndex in
      let start = index(after: fromIndex)
      return suffix(from: start).index(of: toElement)
        .map { toIndex in start..<toIndex }
    }
}
```

Or if you want to go all the way:

```
public func range(between fromElement: Element, and toElement: Element) ->
Range<Index>? {
  return index(of: fromElement)
    .map(index(after: ))
    .map(suffix(from: ))
    .flatMap { suffix in
      suffix.index(of: toElement)
        .map { suffix.startIndex..<$0 }
    }
}
```

reduce

reduce is used to produce a single value from a sequence:

```
func reduce<Result>(_ initialResult: Result, _ nextPartialResult: (Result,
Element) throws -> Result) rethrows -> Result
```

It can be used to, for example, multiply all the numbers together:

```
let multiplied = negative.reduce(1) { result, element in result * element }
```

First, it calls the input function with initialResult and the first element of the sequence. The result is passed to the input function again, together with the next element of the sequence. After going through the entire sequence, the last result from the input function is returned.

There is another version where the result parameter to the input function is inout, in other words, mutable. The input function itself doesn't return anything:

```
func reduce<Result>(into initialResult: Result, _ updateAccumulatingResult:
(inout Result, Self.Element) throws -> ()) rethrows -> Result
```

Here is the previous example using this version:

```
let multiplied2 = negative.reduce(into: 1) { result, element in result =
result * element }
```

The mutable version is best for producing more complex values, such as arrays. It lets us directly add to one array in place instead of having to create a new array for every run of the input function.

Using the reduce Function

Try to use the reduce method yourself in this small exercise:

1. Go to the Exercise - reduce page in Functional.playground. Compute the average using reduce.

Solution:

```
let average = Double(numbers.reduce(0, +)) / Double(numbers.count)
```

Activity: Using Functional Programming

Use Xcode to make part of the code in `CountedSet` from *Lesson 4, Collections* more
functional. We want to make the code clearer, more concise and (hopefully) easier to read.

1. Duplicate the `CollectionsExtra` project from *Lesson 4*, and name the duplicate
    `CollectionsExtraFunc`.

2. Open the new project in Xcode, and go to `CountedSet.swift`.

3. Go to the following method:

    ```
    public var count: Int {
      var result = 0
      for count in elements.values {
        result += count
      }
      return result
    }
    ```

4. This is the archetypical use case for `reduce`. Replace the body of the function with
    this:

    ```
    return elements.values.reduce(0, +)
    ```

    Beautiful, isn't it?

5. Next, go to this function:

    ```
    public mutating func insert<S>(contentsOf other: S)
      where S:Sequence, S.Element == Element {

      for newelement in other {
        insert(newelement)
      }
    }
    ```

6. One option is to use `forEach`:

    ```
    other.forEach({self.insert($0)})
    ```

    Preferably, we would use `other.forEach(insert)` here but it leads to an error
    message about `self` being immutable, even though we are in a mutating method.

    There is a `merge` (`https://developer.apple.com/documentation/swift/`
    `dictionary/2892855-merge`) method on Dictionary that is perfect for us. It takes a
    sequence of key-value pairs and adds it to the dictionary. Every time it encounters
    a key that already exists, it passes the current value and the new one to the function

we provide, and uses whatever that function returns as the new value:

```
elements.merge(other.lazy.map { ($0, 1) }, uniquingKeysWith: +)
```

 The `elements` dictionary has elements for keys and their count as value.

First, we convert the `other` sequence to key-value pairs, which is simple since the count of each element is 1 (we will learn about the `lazy` property in the next section). And for any keys that already exist, we just need to add their values together with the + operator/function.

Lazy Operations

All the sequences and methods we have looked at so far this lesson have been *eager*, which means they perform their operations immediately, and `filter`, `map`, and `flatMap` return their results in arrays. But sometimes, we may want to delay operations until they are needed.

Say you have a very large array, and you want to first use `map` and then perform other operations. If done eagerly, `map` will create a new array with the same number of elements as the original one to store its results. But if we do it lazily, `map` will return a `LazyMapSequence`, which will perform each map operation directly when asked for, without using any intermediate storage.

Infinite sequences *must* be handled lazily, as they obviously cannot be stored.

Lazy Sequences

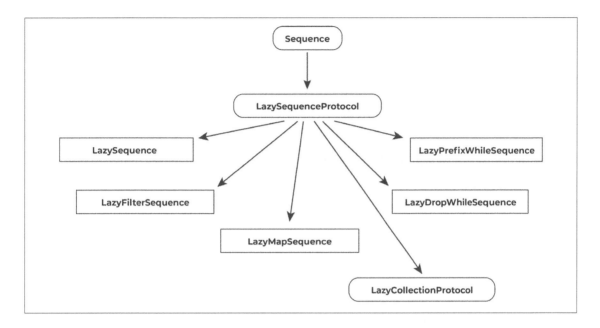

A lazy sequence is one that conforms to `LazySequenceProtocol`. The original sequence itself may or may not work lazily internally, but some further operations on the sequence are lazy, for example, `filter`, `map`, `flatMap`, `drop(while:)`, and `prefix(while:)`.

[Open `Functional.playground` at the `Lazy sequences` page.]

To make a sequence lazy, just use the `lazy` property:

```
let array = [1,2,3,4]
let lazyArray = array.lazy
```

The actual type we get back depends on the type of the original sequence. For array, it is `La zyRandomAccessCollection<Array<Element>>`.

We can chain many operations together:

```
let complexType = lazyArray
  .flatMap { -2..<$0 }
  .map { $0*$0 }
  .filter { $0<4 }
```

Note that none of the operations have been performed yet. This won't happen until we turn the sequence into an array (`Array(complexType)`), use it in a for...in loop, or perform an operation that is not lazy:

```
let eager = complexType.dropFirst(4)
```

One thing you will notice about lazy sequences is that the types may become very long and complex. For example, here is the type signature for `complexType`:

```
LazyFilterCollection<LazyMapCollection<FlattenBidirectionalCollection<LazyM
apBidirectionalCollection<[Int], CountableRange<Int>>>, Int>>
```

If a type signature threatens to get out of hand, we can shorten it with this:

```
let shorterTypeSignature = AnySequence(complexType).lazy
// LazySequence<AnySequence<Int>>
```

Beware that this may prevent some optimizations, as the compiler no longer knows what types are at work.

If they save memory, why not always use lazy sequences?

Because they are not necessarily faster. Lazy operations do not store their results, so every time they are called, they have to do the same operation again. You have to be careful which parts of your chain of operations are lazy to avoid redoing the same operations over and over.

Sequence Internals

[Open `Functional.playground` at the `Sequence internals` page.]

The `Sequence` protocol looks like this (from the Swift source code, slightly simplified; see `https://github.com/apple/swift/blob/master/stdlib/public/core/Sequence.swift`):

```
public protocol Sequence {
    /// A type representing the sequence's elements.
    associatedtype Element

    /// A type that provides the sequence's iteration interface and
    /// encapsulates its iteration state.
    associatedtype Iterator : IteratorProtocol where Iterator.Element ==
Element

    /// Returns an iterator over the elements of this sequence.
    func makeIterator() -> Iterator
}
```

This, of course, begs the question: so what is `IteratorProtocol`?

```
public protocol IteratorProtocol {
    /// The type of element traversed by the iterator.
    associatedtype Element

    /// The next element in the underlying sequence,
    /// if a next element exists; otherwise, `nil`.
    mutating func next() -> Element?
}
```

Every time a sequence is used in a `for...in` loop, or when other methods go through its elements, it first returns an iterator from `makeIterator`, which in turn provides one element at a time from `next`, until it is empty and returns `nil`.

Creating Lazy Operations

 Open `Functional.playground` at the `Lazy operations` page.

How do we create operations that work lazily? For more complex operations, including those that use recursion, it is often best to create a new type which implements the `Sequence` and `IteratorProtocol` protocols. But for simpler tasks, there are two very convenient functions the Standard Library provides.

sequence(first:next:)

`first` is the first value of the sequence, and `next` a function which takes the previous value and returns the next value:

```
func sequence<T>(first: T, next: @escaping (T) -> T?) -> UnfoldSequence<T,
(T?, Bool)>
```

It creates the sequence `first`, `next(first)`, `next(previous element)`, `next(previous element)`, and so on, until `next` returns `nil` (or, if it's infinite, the sequence will continue forever).

It is very useful for following references:

```
for view in sequence(first: someView, next: { $0.superview }) {
  // someView, someView.superview, someView.superview.superview, ...
}
```

It is also useful for some mathematical sequences:

```
let powersOf2 = sequence(first: 1) {
  let result = $0.multipliedReportingOverflow(by: 2)
  return result.overflow ? nil : result.partialValue
}
```

sequence(state:next:)

This function keeps mutable `state` separate from the values it generates:

```
func sequence<T, State>(state: State, next: @escaping (inout State) -> T?)
-> UnfoldSequence<T, State>
```

It creates a sequence by repeatedly passing mutable `state` to the `next` function. It is useful when there are changing values that are different than the output.

Here is the obligatory Fibonacci sequence example (where each element is the sum of the previous two elements):

```
let fibonacci = sequence(state: (0,1)) { numbers -> Int? in
  numbers = (numbers.1, numbers.0 + numbers.1)
  return numbers.0
  }.prefix(91)
```

This outputs 1, 1, 2, 3, 5, 8, and so on. We limit the sequence to the first 91 elements, because the 92nd is too large to fit in an Int type, and the program will crash.

For a slightly more complex example, this method returns the elements of the underlying sequence in groups of two, in tuples:

```
extension LazySequenceProtocol {
  /// Group the elements of this sequence in tuples of 2.
  /// If there is an odd number of elements, the last element is discarded.
  func group2() -> LazySequence<UnfoldSequence<(Element, Element),
Iterator>> {
    return sequence(state: self.makeIterator()) { iterator in
      let result = iterator.next().flatMap { a in
        iterator.next().map { b in (a,b) }
      }
      return result
    }.lazy
  }
}
```

 Ideally we would return directly without using result, but then the compiler complains that *type of expression is ambiguous without more context.*

Here we use the iterator of the underlying sequence as the mutable state, and only return a value if both calls to iterator.next() are not nil. We use flatMap first, because the next line can also be nil.

The code from let result to return result does the same as this:

```
guard let a = iterator.next(),
  let b = iterator.next()
  else { return nil }
return (a,b)
```

Activity: Implementing a Lazy Version of a Method

Use Xcode to make a lazy version of the `allRanges` method from *Lesson 5, Stings*.

We want to make the method use less memory, or be more efficient if we only need some of the ranges.

1. Duplicate the `StringsExtra` project from *Lesson 4, Collections* and name the duplicate `StringsExtraLazy`.

[

If you did not finish the `StringsExtra` project, you can use the project provided for this lesson, and check out the `Activity_B_start_here` branch in the Xcode Source Control Navigator (⌘2).
]

2. Open a new project, and go to `StringsExtra.swift`.
3. First, it would be nice if both the current and the lazy version of the method could be used on both strings and substrings. To achieve this, we must move the current version from `String` to `StringProtocol` (we can do this because the method we use inside, `range(of:)`, is also available on `StringProtocol`). At the top of the file, change the line `extension String {` to `extension StringProtocol {`.
4. We get an error message a couple of lines below, saying this:

```
Cannot convert value of type 'Range<Self.Index>' to expected argument
type 'Range<String.Index>'
```

This is because even though only String and Substring conform to `StringProtocol`, and they both use `String.Index` as index type, this associated type has not been set on `StringProtocol`. We need to constrain our extension:

```
extension StringProtocol where Index == String.Index {
```

5. There is still one error in `countLinguisticTokens`. We won't deal with that now, but just move that method to the extension on String below.

6. Run unit tests, and verify that they pass.

7. At the bottom of the file, add the following:

```
extension LazySequenceProtocol where Elements: StringProtocol, Elements.
Index == String.Index {


}
```

    Here, we are adding the same constraints as in the preceding extension, except we add them to `LazySequenceProtocol.Elements`.

8. Paste a copy of the original `allRanges` method into the new extension. Some errors appear:

```
Use of unresolved identifier 'startIndex'
Use of unresolved identifier 'endIndex'
```

    This is because we are no longer in String. We are in `LazySequenceProtocol`, and it does not have those properties. However, its `elements` property is a string or a substring, thanks to the constraints we added to the extension. So, for every error that now appears, insert `elements.` in front of the identifier mentioned in the error message, for example:

```
    var searchRange = searchRange ?? startIndex..<endIndex
```

    Becomes:

```
    var searchRange = searchRange ?? elements.startIndex..<elements.
endIndex
```

9. Verify that everything builds okay (⌘ + *B*).

10. Now, let's look at the method and how to make it lazy. We will be returning a sequence of some kind, but we're not quite sure which yet. For now, we can just remove the return type from the function definition, and the `return` statement at the end. We no longer need the `ranges` variable; remove the two lines it appears in.

11. We should now be left with this:

```
extension LazySequenceProtocol where Elements: StringProtocol, Elements.
Index == String.Index {
  public func allRanges(of aString: String,
    options: String.CompareOptions = [],
    range searchRange: Range<String.Index>? = nil,
    locale: Locale? = nil) {

    var searchRange = searchRange ?? elements.startIndex ..< elements.
endIndex

    while let foundRange = self.elements.range(
      of: aString, options: options,
      range: searchRange, locale: locale) {

      searchRange = options.contains(.backwards) ?
        searchRange.lowerBound ..< self.elements.index(before:
foundRange.upperBound) :
        self.elements.index(after: foundRange.lowerBound) ..<
searchRange.upperBound
    }
  }
}
```

The code inside the `while` loop is what will be run for each turn of the sequence we are creating. We need to identify what state is changing each time. In this case, it is easy to see, as `searchRange` is the only variable left.

12. So, we have some state external to the loop; the `sequence(state:)` function seems like a good fit. Insert this on the line above the `while` loop:

```
let result =
```

13. Begin to type `seq`, and select `sequence(state:` (and so on) from the auto completion pop-up menu. Enter `searchRange` in the first blue field, press *Tab*, and then press enter on the next blue field. You are left with this:

```
let result = sequence(state: searchRange) { () -> T? in

}
```

14. We can just name the input parameter to the closure `searchRange` as well, and the return type, the element type of the sequence we are now creating, is `Range<String.Index>`:

```
let result = sequence(state: searchRange) {
    (searchRange) -> Range<String.Index>? in
}
```

15. Move the closing brace down so the entire loop is inside the closure. Ignore the *Missing return in a closure...* error message.

16. We need to know when to stop, and that is when `foundRange` is `nil`. Change the `while let` line and the next two lines to this:

```
guard let foundRange = self.elements.range(
    of: aString, options: options,
    range: searchRange, locale: locale)
    else { return nil }
```

17. Now we can listen to the error message; insert this at the end of the closure:

```
return foundRange
```

18. There should be a warning on the first line of the body of the method. Click on it, and then click on **fix** to change `var searchRange` to `let searchRange`.

19. Now all that is left is to actually return something from the method. Click on `result` to put the text marker inside it, and look in the Quick Help Inspector in the top-right corner of the window (if it is not already open, press ⌘⌥2). You should see the type of the sequence there. Click on **UnfoldSequence** to view the documentation:

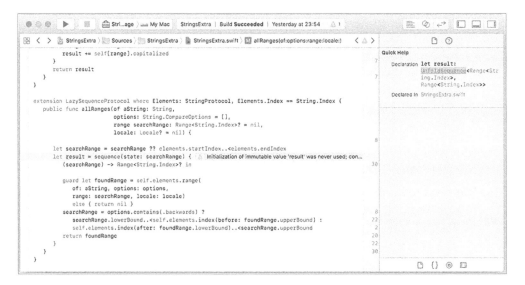

20. Go to the bottom of the documentation page, where it says this:

```
Conforms To IteratorProtocol, Sequence
```

`UnfoldSequence` performs its operations lazily and internally, but since it does not conform to `LazySequenceProtocol`, other operations on it like `map` and `filter` are not lazy. Since we are adding a method to `LazySequenceProtocol`, we need to make sure that any sequence we return also conforms to it. To do this, add `.lazy` right after the closing brace of the closure, on the line below `return foundRange`.

21. Place the text marker inside `result` again. In the top right corner, the type has changed to this:

```
LazySequence<UnfoldSequence<Range<String.Index>, Range<String.Index>>>
```

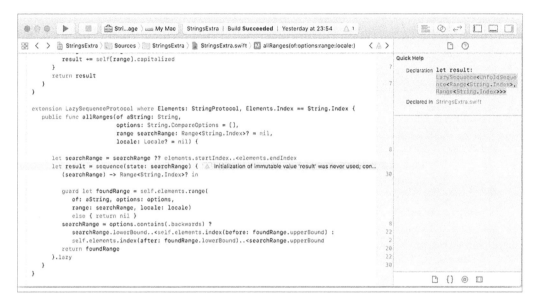

Copy and paste it in as the return type of the method.

22. Replace `let result` `=` with `return`.

23. Verify that it builds.

24. Go to the unit test file `StringsExtraTests.swift`, and insert the following below the first unit test:

```swift
func testAllRangesLazy() {
    let lazyString = string.lazy

    XCTAssertEqual(Array(lazyString.allRanges(of: "Line", options:
.caseInsensitive)).count, 2)
    XCTAssertEqual(Array(lazyString.allRanges(of: "Line")).count, 1)
    XCTAssertEqual(Array(lazyString.allRanges(of: "hsf")).count, 0)
    XCTAssertEqual(Array("LineLineLine".lazy.allRanges(of: "Line")).
count, 3)
    XCTAssertEqual(Array("lalalalalala".lazy.allRanges(of: "lala")).
count, 5)
    XCTAssertEqual(Array("llllllll".lazy.allRanges(of: "ll")).count, 7)
    XCTAssertEqual(Array(lazyString.allRanges(
        of: "li", options: .caseInsensitive, locale: .current).
map{string[$0]}).count, 2)
    XCTAssertEqual(Array(lazyString.allRanges(
        of: "li", options: [.caseInsensitive, .backwards], locale:
.current)).count, 2)
}
```

Here, we extract all elements from the lazy sequences by wrapping them in arrays.

25. Run all unit tests (⌘U) and verify that they all pass.

And that's it. Congratulations!

Swifty Code

When learning a new programming language, you're not just learning syntax, built-in libraries, tooling, terminology, formatting style, and so on. There is also a somewhat vaguely defined idea of what constitutes *good code*, a way of performing some tasks that fits well with the language and has evolved together with it over time. In Swift, such code is often referred to as *Swifty* code. This is in no way a well-defined term, and experts in the language may disagree on some points. Here, we will only cover things where there seems to be a consensus. The list is by no means exhaustive, and there are exceptions to many of these.

Many of these points are covered in Apple's official guidelines (https://swift.org/documentation/api-design-guidelines/). We strongly recommend reading it; it's a fairly short page and a very easy read.

Naming

Names of types and protocols are in UpperCamelCase. Everything else is in lowerCamelCase. This makes it easy to tell values and types apart.

Try to name functions and their parameters so that they form English phrases when called. So, instead of this:

```
x.insert(y, position: z)
x.subViews(color: y)
x.nounCapitalize()
```

Do this:

```
x.insert(y, at: z)
x.subViews(havingColor: y)
x.capitalizingNouns()
```

Functions returning Booleans should read well in an `if` statement:

```
if x.isEmpty {...}
if line1.intersects(line2) {...}
```

Methods that are mutating or have other side effects should read like commands:

```
print(x), x.sort(), x.append(y)
```

If this isn't possible because the operation is best described by a noun, prepend `form` instead:

```
y.formUnion(z), c.formSuccessor(&i)
```

Append `ed` or `ing` to methods that return a new value instead of mutating:

Mutating	Nonmutating
`x.sort()`	`z = x.sorted()`
`x.append(y)`	`z = x.appending(y)`

For nouns, just use the noun on its own for the non-mutating version:

Mutating	Nonmutating
`y.formUnion(z)`	`x = y.union(z)`
`c.formSuccessor(&i)`	`j = c.successor(i)`

Organizing Code

Avoid free functions, and place them where they belong. A function that processes text should be placed in an extension on `StringProtocol` (so it can be used by both strings and substrings). If the function doesn't take a value as input, make it static.

Group methods and properties that belong together in one extension. For example, if you are adding protocol conformance to a type, group everything that is required by that protocol together in one extension.

If you have a function that is only going to be used from one other function, place it inside that function. This makes it clear why it exists.

Miscellaneous

Don't put semicolons at the end of lines. That is pointless in Swift. You can, however, use a semicolon to write two statements on one line, but that is not something you should do very often.

Languages without optionals have various ways of signaling the absence of a value: `""` for strings, `-1` for positive integers, `null` for objects, and so on. Swift, thankfully, only has one – `nil`. Always use optionals if a value can be empty.

Use `Int` for most integers, even if you only need positive values or smaller values that can fit in Int8, Int16, or Int32. Otherwise, you will have to do a lot of conversions since Swift does not do this automatically, not even when it is guaranteed to be safe.

Unless the order is significant, place a parameter taking a closure last in the function definition so that it can be used with trailing closure syntax. Place parameters with default values second to last.

Put underscores in long numeric literals, so they are easier to read:

```
1_000_000, 0.352_463
```

If you need to change a value after you have returned it, don't do this:

```
let oldvalue = value
value += 1
return oldvalue
```

Use `defer` instead:

```
defer { value += 1 }
return value
```

Writing Swifty Code

Finally, we're ready to write Swifty code.

1. Rewrite the following code to be more Swifty, using the guidelines mentioned previously:

```
/// An immutable entry in an error log.
struct LogError {
  var header: String
  let errorMessage: String

  init(header: String = "", errorMessage: String) {
    self.header = header
    self.errorMessage = errorMessage;
    if header.isEmpty {
      self.header = " ::Error::errorCode::"
    }
  }
}

LogError(errorMessage: "something bad")
LogError(header: "head", errorMessage: "something bad")
```

One solution:

```
/// An immutable entry in an error log.
struct ErrorLogItem {
  let header: String
  let errorMessage: String

  init(errorMessage: String, header: String? = nil) {
    // Only if empty strings are invalid as headers.
    precondition(header != "", "A header cannot be empty.")

    self.header = header ?? " ::Error::errorCode::"
    self.errorMessage = errorMessage
  }
}

ErrorLogItem(errorMessage: "something bad")
ErrorLogItem(errorMessage: "something bad", header: "head")
```

This ends our brief journey into code naming and organization, or in other words, how to write code in a *Swifty* way.

Summary

In this lesson, we learned about the functional operations `filter`, `map`, `flatMap`, and `reduce`. Then, we learned about lazy operations and a few ways of creating them. Finally, we learned characteristics of good Swifty code.

The last three lessons of this course have been focused on the Swift Standard Library. We began with learning about the three main generic collections: Arrays, Sets, and Dictionaries, and added some useful methods to them. We also created our own collection: `CountedSet`. Then, we learned about text handling in Swift and working with Foundation, and added some useful String methods. We also looked at functional programming and lazy operations.

This entire course is designed to be a thorough introduction to Swift for programmers who are new to the language. We hope you have found it useful and welcome you as a fellow Swift programmer.

Further Study

Apple's own books on Swift programming (`https://itunes.apple.com/no/book-series/swift-programming-series/id888896989?mt=11`) are very well-written and highly recommended. So are the books from the no-longer-appropriately-named objc.io (`https://www.objc.io/books/`).

Challenge

Here's the final challenge; the Standard Library has methods for splitting a string over a single character, or a function that takes a single character and returns a Boolean. However, it doesn't have any methods for splitting a string over a substring, or doing it lazily.

Create a new method, which can be used on lazy strings and substrings, and takes a separator (String) and optionally `String.CompareOptions` and `Locale`, and returns a lazy sequence of the ranges between each occurrence of the separator in the original string/substring.

There are several ways of achieving this. The following hints describe one solution which uses some of the methods we have created in this course. Try and see if you can complete this by using as few hints as possible.

Hints:

- We can find the ranges of the separators first, and then *invert* them to get the ranges of the spaces between the separators.

- Use the lazy `allranges` method we created in *Lesson 6*.

- Break up the `lowerBound` and `upperBound` of the ranges of the separators into a sequence of indices.

- Create a new sequence, still lazy, from the start index of the original string/substring, the indices from the previous hint, and the end index.

- There is no built-in way of joining sequences of different types lazily together. Here is one way:

```
private func joinSequences<S1,S2>(_ s1: S1, _ s2: S2)
    -> UnfoldSequence<S1.Element, (Optional<S1.Iterator>, S2.Iterator)>
    where S1:Sequence, S2:Sequence, S1.Element == S2.Element {
      return sequence(state: (Optional(s1.makeIterator()),
s2.makeIterator()))
        { seqs -> S1.Element? in
          guard let _ = seqs.0 else { return seqs.1.next() }
          return seqs.0?.next()
            ?? { seqs.0 = nil; return seqs.1.next() }()
        }
}


public func +<S1,S2>(s1: S1, s2: S2)
    -> UnfoldSequence<S1.Element, (Optional<S1.Iterator>, S2.Iterator)>
    where S1:Sequence, S2:Sequence, S1.Element == S2.Element {
      return joinSequences(s1, s2)
}


public func +<S1,S2>(s1: S1, s2: S2)
    -> LazySequence<UnfoldSequence<S1.Element, (Optional<S1.Iterator>,
S2.Iterator)>>
    where S1:Sequence, S2:LazySequenceProtocol, S1.Element == S2.Element {
      return joinSequences(s1, s2).lazy
}


public func +<S1,S2>(s1: S1, s2: S2)
```

```
    -> LazySequence<UnfoldSequence<S1.Element, (Optional<S1.Iterator>,
S2.Iterator)>>
    where S1:LazySequenceProtocol, S2:Sequence, S1.Element == S2.Element {
        return joinSequences(s1, s2).lazy
}
```

- Take the new sequence, flatten it if necessary, and group two and two indices together.

- Use the `group2` method from *Lesson 6*.

- Create ranges from these grouped indices.

- Return this as a lazy sequence.

Index

Lightning Source UK Ltd.
Milton Keynes UK
UKHW032056120320
360268UK00009B/237

9 781789 534313